Machines

PRENTICE HALL GENERAL REFERENCE
15 Columbus Circle
New York, New York 10023

Copyright © 1993 by Merlion Publishing Ltd.

All rights reserved including the right of reproduction in whole or
in part in any form.

PRENTICE HALL and colophon are registered trademarks of
Simon & Schuster Inc.

Library of Congress Cataloging in Publication data

ISBN 0–671–84696–5

Designed by Steven Hulbert
Manufactured in Great Britain by BPCC Hazells Ltd.

Originally published in Great Britain by Merlion Publishing Ltd. as
THE ILLUSTRATED DICTIONARY OF MACHINES in a different
form.

A Prentice Hall Illustrated Dictionary

Machines

Contributors
Michael Pollard
Merilyn Holme

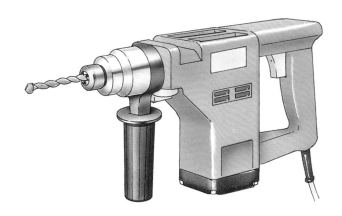

PRENTICE HALL GENERAL REFERENCE
New York · London · Toronto · Sydney · Tokyo · Singapore

Reader's notes

The entries in this dictionary have several features to help you broaden your understanding of the word you are looking up.

- Each entry is introduced by its headword. All the headwords in the dictionary are arranged in alphabetical order.

- Each headword is followed by a part of speech to show whether the word is used as a noun, adjective, verb, or prefix.

- Each entry begins with a sentence that uses the headword as its subject.

- Words that are bold in an entry are cross references. You can look them up in this dictionary to find out more information about the topic.

- The sentence in italics at the end of an entry helps you to see how the headword can be used.

- Many of the entries are accompanied by illustrations. The labels on the illustrations highlight the key points of information and will help you to understand some of the science behind the entries.

- Many of the labels on the illustrations have their own entries in the dictionary and can therefore be used as cross references.

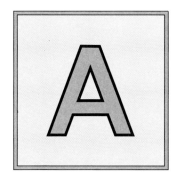

accelerate   *verb*
Accelerate is a word which describes an increase in speed. An object accelerates when a **force** makes it move faster.
The car accelerated around the last bend, along the straight and won the race.
acceleration   *noun*

accelerator   *noun*
1. An accelerator is a pedal or **lever** that releases the **power** of an **engine** and makes it run faster.
The driver put his foot on the accelerator and caught up with the car in front.
2. An accelerator is a **machine** that greatly increases the speed of subatomic particles of matter by giving them an electric charge. It is used to break up atoms.
Accelerators are used in medicine and industry.

accelerometer   *noun*
An accelerometer is a **device** that measures the rate at which a **machine's** speed increases. It shows the measurement on a **dial**.
The jet plane's accelerometer showed how its speed increased as it dived toward the ground.

aerial   *adjective*
Aerial describes an object that travels through the air, such as an **airplane**. It also describes an activity that is carried out in the air, such as aerial photography.
The aircraft carried out an aerial survey of the coastline.

aerial   *noun*
An aerial is a long piece of wire, a rod or a dish that transmits or receives radio signals. An aerial is connected to a **transmitter** or a **receiver**. It is also called an **antenna**.
A radio receives signals through its aerial and changes them into sounds that we can recognize.

aerosol   *noun*
An aerosol is a fine mist of liquid or powder. The mist is sprayed out of a can by pressing a button. This kind of can is often called an aerosol, too.
She used an aerosol to kill the flies in the kitchen.

aerodynamics   *noun*
Aerodynamics is the science that deals with the forces of air on moving objects.
The engineers used the principles of aerodynamics to design a more efficient automobile.

aerometer   *noun*
An aerometer is an instrument for measuring the density of air and other gases.
The aerometer showed that the sample of helium in the beaker was lighter than the sample of air.

afterburner   *noun*
An afterburner is a **machine** that sprays **fuel** into the **exhaust** pipe of a **jet engine** to give the engine extra **power**.
The fighter pilot used his afterburners to increase his speed.

afterburner

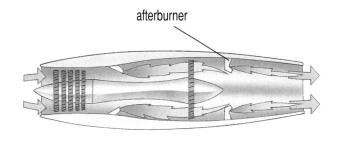

aileron *noun*
An aileron is a hinged flap on the rear edge of each wing of an **airplane**.
Ailerons make a plane turn left or right.

air cleaner *noun*
An air cleaner is a **machine** that removes harmful **chemicals** and dust from **gases** produced by factories and **power stations**.
Air cleaners help to prevent air pollution.

air conditioner *noun*
An air conditioner is a **machine** that cools the air in a building. It pumps away stale, hot air and replaces it with clean, cool air. Air conditioners can also be used in **automobiles** and other **vehicles**.
The office was fresh and cool in summer because it had an air conditioner.

aircraft ► page 8

airfoil *noun*
An airfoil is a curved surface that is held up, or supported, by the flow of air around it. Airfoils help **aircraft** to stay in the air and to change direction.
Air flows more quickly over the top of an airfoil than underneath it.

air hammer *noun*
An air hammer is a **pneumatic machine**. It uses **compressed air** to push the **hammer** head down.
The factory was noisy with the sound of air hammers.

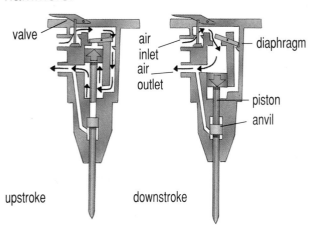

valve   air inlet   diaphragm
air outlet   piston   anvil
upstroke   downstroke

air ionizer *noun*
An air ionizer is a **machine** that removes **electrons** from negatively charged atoms (negative ions) in the air to make them positively charged (positive ions). An air ionizer is used in a room where there is a lot of electrical equipment.
The air ionizer helped to prevent the computer room from feeling stuffy.

airliner *noun*
An airliner is an **airplane** designed to carry passengers. Airliners fly on regular routes between one airport and another.
The Concorde is a supersonic airliner that flies at speeds faster than sound.

airplane *noun*
An airplane is an **aircraft** with one or more pairs of wings. Fighters, bombers and **airliners** are all airplanes.
We flew by airplane when we went on vacation.

airport crash tender *noun*
An airport crash tender is a **vehicle** that is on duty whenever **aircraft** take off or land at an airport. It has **firefighting** and other equipment for use in an emergency.
The airplane landed on one engine and the airport crash tender rushed to the scene.

airship *noun*
An airship is an **aircraft**. Its cabin and **engine** are slung beneath a huge balloon filled with a light **gas** called helium. The balloon is stretched over an **aluminum** frame. An airship can fly because the gas inside it is lighter, or less dense, than air.
Airships use tall structures called mooring towers to take off and land.

airspeed indicator *noun*
An airspeed indicator is an instrument on the **control panel** of an **aircraft**. It shows how fast the aircraft is traveling through the air.
The pilot checked the airspeed indicator to see if the aircraft would arrive on time.

alarm system *noun*
An alarm system is a **device** that gives warning of dangers such as fire or intruders usually by sounding a bell or siren. Alarm systems use electronic **sensors** to keep a constant check for danger.
The alarm system was set off by someone climbing over the factory wall.

alcohol breath tester *noun*
An alcohol breath tester is a small **device** that is used by police to check whether a driver has been drinking too much alcohol. The driver breathes into a tube, and the tester shows how much alcohol is in the driver's blood.
The alcohol breath tester showed that she was unfit to drive.

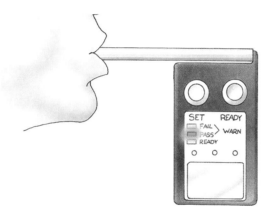

alloy *noun*
An alloy is a mixture of metals or other materials. It is made by melting two or more kinds of material together. Alloys are often stronger than the materials they are made from, and stand up to heat better.
Alloys are used for many parts of jet engines.

alternating current *noun*
Alternating current is a flow of **electricity** that behaves in a special way. It grows stronger and then weaker and then changes direction. This takes place many times every second.
The electricity supply in most homes is alternating current.

alternator *noun*
An alternator is a **machine** that produces, or generates, **alternating current**. The **shaft** of the alternator is made to spin at great speed and is surrounded by a magnet.
Most power stations contain alternators that are driven by steam turbines.

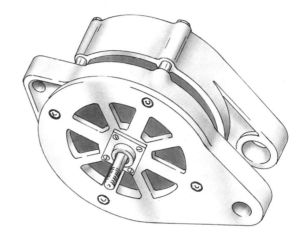

altimeter *noun*
An altimeter is an instrument on the **control panel** of an **aircraft**. It shows how high the aircraft is flying by measuring the weight of air pressing around the aircraft. This weight of air is called the atmospheric pressure.
The pilot looked at the altimeter to see whether she had reached her planned altitude.

aluminum *noun*
Aluminum is a soft, silvery metal that is light in weight. It is taken out, or extracted, from an ore called bauxite, when bauxite is heated.
Aluminum is used for making an aircraft's fuselage and wings.

amplifier *noun*
An amplifier is a **device** that changes a weak **electric signal** into a stronger one. It also cuts out unwanted sounds that sometimes come from disturbance in the atmosphere. Most amplifiers use **transistors** linked by **electric circuits**.
Radios and stereo systems contain amplifiers.
amplify *verb*

aircraft *noun*

An aircraft is any kind of **machine** that travels by air. It may have wings like an **airplane** or rotor blades like a **helicopter**, or it may be an **airship**.

We saw many different kinds of aircraft at the airport.

A large passenger airplane has four powerful jet engines. It can carry more than 500 passengers at a speed of 600 miles per hour. The airplane can travel thousands of miles without having to take on more fuel.

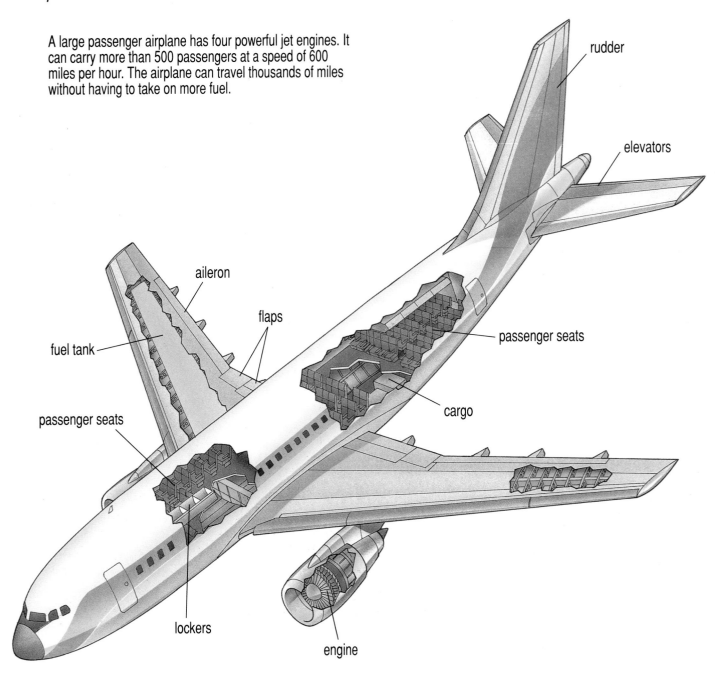

rudder

elevators

aileron

flaps

passenger seats

fuel tank

cargo

passenger seats

lockers

engine

A helicopter is powered by two spinning blades called rotors.

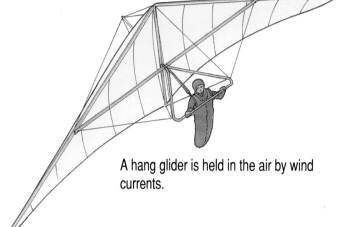

A hang glider is held in the air by wind currents.

An airship has a large balloon, or envelope, filled with helium gas and shaped like an airfoil.

A glider looks like an airplane, but it is powered by the wind instead of an engine.

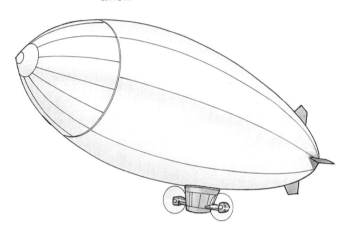

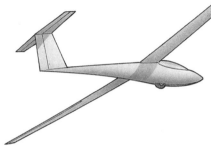

How an airplane flies

An airplane wing is shaped like an airfoil. As the air pushes over the curved, upper surface of the wing, its pressure drops. The air under the wing moves more slowly, so its pressure stays higher. It pushes the airplane up into the air and holds it there.

An airplane needs powerful engines to give it enough thrust to overcome its weight and the drag of the fuselage and wings.

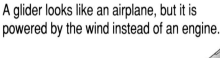

lift

airflow

air pressure drops

wing

air pressure stays the same

direction of flight

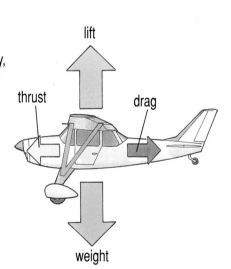

lift

thrust

drag

weight

analogue   *adjective*
Analogue describes something that is like, or similar to, something else. It applies to **machines** that copy the way things work in real life. A **watch** with a **dial** and hands is an analogue watch. Its hands copy the movement of Earth around the Sun. A watch that shows only numerals is called a **digital** watch.
The minute hand of an analogue clock takes one hour to move around the dial.

anchor escapement   *noun*
An anchor escapement is part of a clockwork **watch** or **clock**. It rocks to and fro and controls the unwinding of the **spring**. This makes the hands of the clock tick forward. There is a tooth on each arm of the anchor escapement that connects with a **cog wheel**.
The anchor escapement gets its name from its shape, which is like a ship's anchor.

anemometer   *noun*
An anemometer is an instrument for measuring the speed of the wind. The most common type of anemometer is made up of three or four cups mounted on a pole. When the anemometer is placed in an open space, the wind drives the cups around, and a counter **mechanism** in the instrument records how fast the cups spin. The wind speed is then shown on a display panel.
The anemometer showed that the wind was blowing a full gale.

aneroid barometer   *noun*
An aneroid barometer is an instrument for measuring atmospheric pressure. It has a thin, round, metal box that contains a partial **vacuum**. The pressure of the air outside makes the sides of the box move in or out. A needle shows this movement on a **dial**.
The aneroid barometer showed that the atmospheric pressure was high, so it would be a sunny day.

antenna   *noun*
Antenna is another name for an **aerial**.
The receiver's antenna picked up the radio signals.

anvil   *noun*
An anvil is a block of **iron** or **steel** that is used to shape metal objects. One end is shaped like an oblong block, the other like a cone.
The blacksmith hammered the horseshoe on the anvil.

aperture   *noun*
An aperture is a hole or an opening. The **lens** of a **camera** has an aperture through which light passes. The light entering the aperture makes an image on the film inside the camera.
In most cameras, the size of the aperture can be changed to let different amounts of light through.

appliance   ▶ page 12

aqualung *noun*
An aqualung is a piece of equipment that divers use to breathe under water. It has metal tanks of **compressed air**, which the diver inhales through a tube and **valve**.
The diver adjusted the mouthpiece of his aqualung so that he could breathe more easily.

Archimedes' screw *noun*
Archimedes' screw is a method of raising water from one level to another. A screw-shaped channel turns inside a hollow **shaft** and carries the water upward. It was invented by Archimedes, a Greek scientist who lived more than 2,000 years ago.
Archimedes' screw is still used in some places to water fields where crops are grown.

arc lamp *noun*
An arc lamp is a **device** that produces a very bright light. An **electric current** passes across the space between two carbon rods. The rods become white hot and glow very brightly.
Some of the first arc lamps were used in lighthouses.

asbestos *noun*
Asbestos is a mineral. It can be separated into fibers and then woven into sheets. It can also be mixed with material such as rubber or cement. Asbestos does not burn and can be used to protect people and objects against heat. Breathing asbestos dust is very harmful, and for this reason asbestos is rarely used today.
Firefighters sometimes wear asbestos suits to protect them from the heat of a fire.

asphalt *noun*
Asphalt is a mixture of a black, tarry substance called bitumen with gravel or sand. It melts when heated. Asphalt is used to pave road surfaces.
The road workers gave the highway a new covering of asphalt.

assembly line ► page 14

auto- *prefix*
Auto- is a prefix that describes a **machine** that controls itself. An automatic machine does not need a person to control it.
Newscasters read the news on television with the help of an automatic machine called an autocue, or teleprompter.

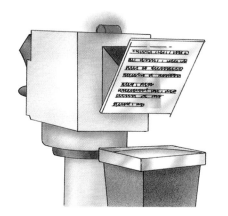

autocue

automatic governor *noun*
An automatic governor is a **device** that controls the speed of a **machine**. It controls the amount of **fuel** used, so that if the machine starts to run too fast, the automatic governor slows it down to the correct speed.
The automatic governor kept the machine running at an even speed.

automatic machine *noun*
An automatic machine is a **machine** that works without human help.
A vending machine that sells drinks or candy is an automatic machine.

automation *noun*
Automation is a system used in some factories, where work is done entirely by **machines**. **Computers** usually control the machines.
There are only a few workers in this factory because most of the work is done by automation.

appliance   *noun*

An appliance is a **machine** used for a special purpose. **Washing machines** and **food processors** are household appliances. *A vacuum cleaner is an appliance that most people have in their homes.*

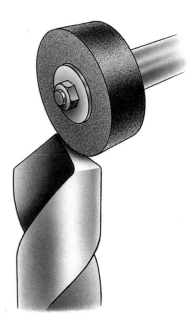

A grinding wheel polishes and sharpens a metal surface.

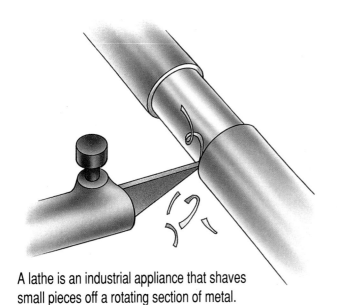

A lathe is an industrial appliance that shaves small pieces off a rotating section of metal.

A saw cuts metal to a certain size.

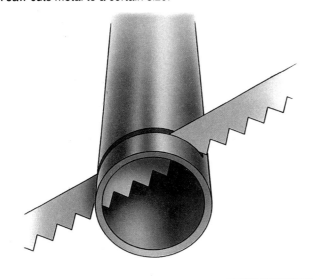

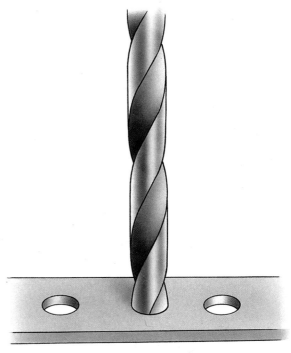

A drill makes holes in a strip, sheet, or block of metal.

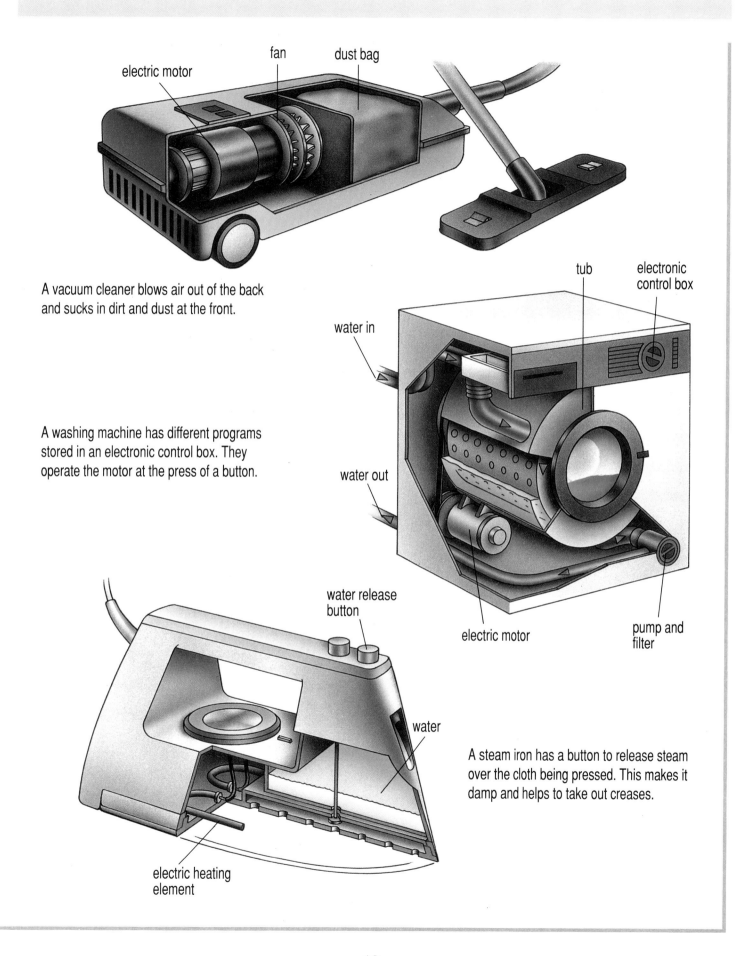

electric motor   fan   dust bag

A vacuum cleaner blows air out of the back and sucks in dirt and dust at the front.

A washing machine has different programs stored in an electronic control box. They operate the motor at the press of a button.

tub   electronic control box

water in

water out

electric motor   pump and filter

water release button

water

electric heating element

A steam iron has a button to release steam over the cloth being pressed. This makes it damp and helps to take out creases.

assembly line   *noun*

An assembly line is a row of **machines** found in many factories. Each machine carries out a different stage in the manufacturing process. Many machines in an assembly line are worked by **computers** or **robots**. **Products** as small as a personal stereo or as large as a tractor are produced on an assembly line.

Cars are built on an assembly line.

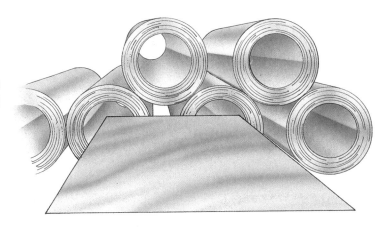

A sheet of steel is made ready for shaping into the body of a car.

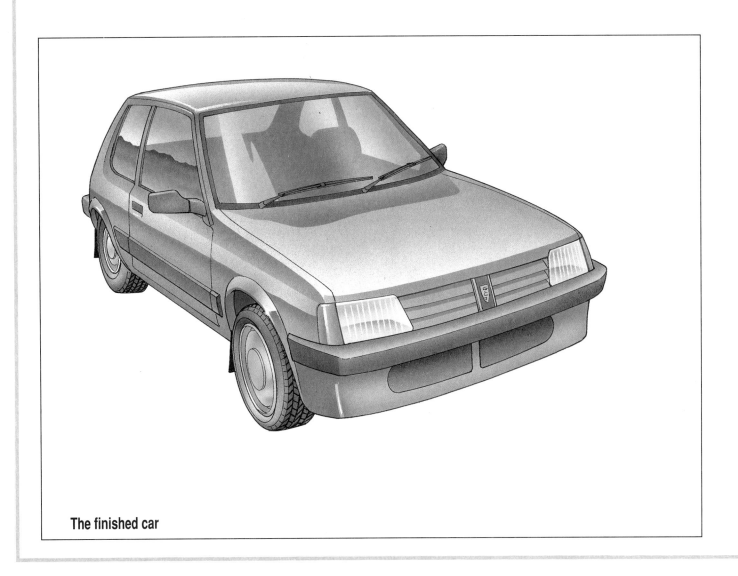

The finished car

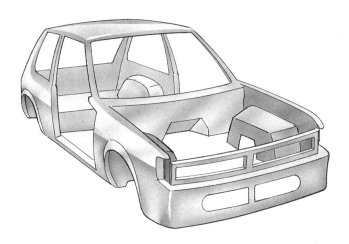

All the sections of the car body have been cut, pressed into shape and put together, or assembled. The body is dipped in a fluid to protect it against rust. Then it is given a coat of primer paint.

The car body is sprayed with paint. Then such parts as the wheels, windshield, and fuse box are installed.

The engine is tested carefully before it is installed in the car. All the inside parts, such as the seats and carpeting, are also put in at this stage.

The windows, bumpers, and wheels are covered before the car is given its final painting.

automobile   *noun*
An automobile is a road **vehicle**. It is powered by an **internal combustion engine**. Most automobiles burn **gasoline** in their engines, but some use **diesel fuel**.
The family went on vacation in their automobile.

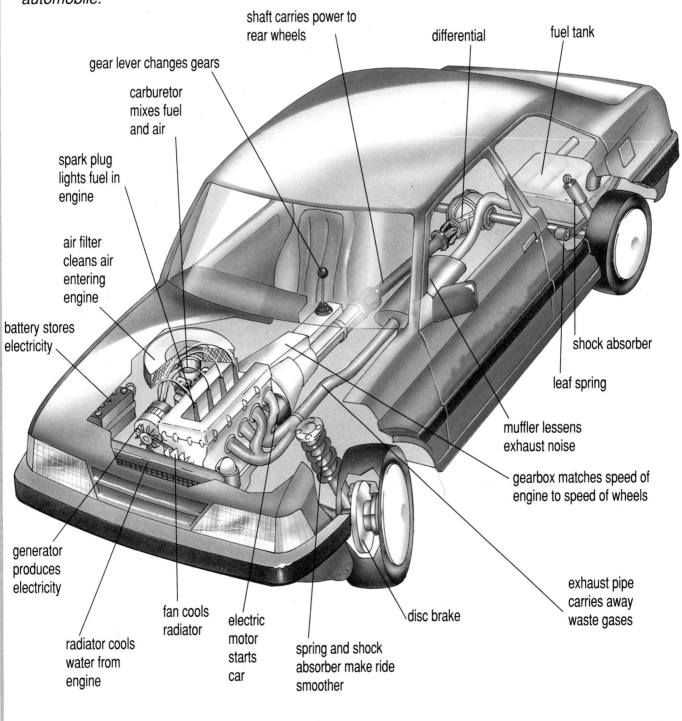

shaft carries power to rear wheels

differential

fuel tank

gear lever changes gears

carburetor mixes fuel and air

spark plug lights fuel in engine

air filter cleans air entering engine

battery stores electricity

shock absorber

leaf spring

muffler lessens exhaust noise

gearbox matches speed of engine to speed of wheels

generator produces electricity

fan cools radiator

electric motor starts car

disc brake

exhaust pipe carries away waste gases

radiator cools water from engine

spring and shock absorber make ride smoother

Karl Benz's Patent Motor Car, 1886, had a top speed of less than 10 miles per hour.

The Ford Model T, 1915, was built on an assembly line in the United States.

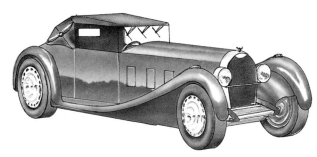

The Bugatti Royale, 1927, was the longest car ever made. It had a 12.7-liter engine and a top speed of more than 100 miles per hour.

The Jaguar XK120 of 1948 was the first of a new kind of streamlined sports car. Its engine design is still used today.

The German Volkswagen Beetle was first made in 1945. It is one of the most popular cars of all time.

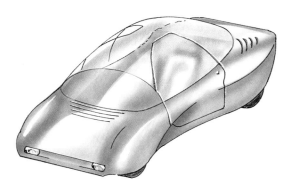

A car of the future will have a sleek, streamlined body and may run on electricity or solar power.

automobile ▶ page 16

autopilot *noun*
An autopilot is a **machine** on the flight deck of an **airplane** that automatically controls the direction in which the airplane flies. It has **gyroscopic sensors** that control the aircraft's movements.
The captain of the airliner set the autopilot to fly the airplane due south.

axle *noun*
An axle is a rod that fits into the center of a **wheel** so that the wheel can turn, or revolve, around it.
A wheelbarrow has one wheel on a very short axle.

baggage scanner *noun*
A baggage scanner is a **machine** that allows people to see what is inside a closed suitcase or bag. **X-rays** are used to make the contents appear on a **television** screen. Baggage scanners are used at airports and at other security centers.
The baggage scanner showed that there was a gun inside the suitcase.

balance *noun*
A balance is a **weighing machine**. Some balances work by stretching a **spring**. Others have a beam, balanced in the center. The object to be weighed is attached to one end, and a known weight, such as a pound, is attached to the other.
The scientist used a balance to find the weight of one grain of sand.
balance *verb*

baler *noun*
A baler is a **machine** that makes bundles, or bales, out of such material as straw or waste paper. It ties the bundles so that they can be moved easily. The bundles are usually rectangular in shape.
After the wheat had been harvested, a baler made the straw into bales.

ball bearing *noun*
A ball bearing is a part of some **machines**. It is made from two steel rings that fit one inside the other. The rings are kept apart by steel balls. When the two rings move, the balls also move and reduce **friction**.
Bicycles have ball bearings in the hubs of their wheels.

ballcock *noun*
A ballcock is a **device** that controls the flow of liquids. It floats on the surface of the liquid. When the container is nearly full, a **valve** attached to the ballcock shuts off the supply.
The ballcock prevents the cold water tank from overflowing.

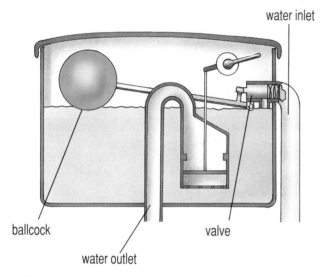

water inlet

ballcock

water outlet

valve

ballpoint pen *noun*
A ballpoint pen is a kind of pen with a ball at its point. Ink flows from inside the pen over the surface of the ball, leaving a mark where the pen is moved over the paper.
He used a ballpoint pen to write smoothly on the paper.

bar code *noun*
A bar code is a pattern of thick and thin lines printed on the packages of items sold in stores. The code is read by a **laser scanner** or a **light pen**, which passes information to a **computer**.
Some libraries use bar codes to keep track of people who borrow books.

barometer *noun*
A barometer is an instrument that measures atmospheric pressure, which is the weight of the air pressing down on Earth. Barometers help us to forecast the weather.
When the barometer shows that the pressure is lower than normal, it means it may rain.

BASIC *noun*
BASIC is a **computer** language. The name BASIC comes from the initial letters of Beginner's All-purpose Symbolic Instruction Code.
The computer program he was using was written in BASIC.

bathroom scale *noun*
A bathroom scale is a **weighing machine**. People stand on a platform to check their weight, which is shown on a **dial** or in **digital** numbers.
The bathroom scale showed that he had gained one pound in the past week.

bathyscaph *noun*
A bathyscaph is an underwater **vessel** used by deep-sea explorers. It is made of thick, strong metals so that it can withstand the strong water pressure found deep under the sea. A bathyscaph can go as deep as seven miles.
The scientists went down to the ocean floor in a bathyscaph.

battery *noun*
A battery is a **device** that supplies an **electric current**. It turns **chemical** energy into electrical energy. Some **watches** and **calculators** have tiny batteries. Motor **vehicles** have large, powerful batteries.
There was no energy left in the batteries in her radio, so she bought new ones.

beam engine   *noun*
A beam engine is a **machine** that is used for pumping water. Its beam makes a seesaw motion when the **engine** is working. The beam connects the **piston** with the **pump mechanism**.
Beam engines were once used to pump water from coal mines.

bell ► **electric bell**

bellows   *plural noun*
Bellows make up a **device** used to create a stream of air. They have sides like an accordion, which the user presses together with handles. The air inside the bellows is then forced out through a nozzle in the front.
She used bellows to blow air on the fire that she had just started.

bevel gear   *noun*
A bevel gear is a **device** that has two **gear wheels** set at an angle to each other. When the teeth move together, the direction of the driving force is changed from one angle to the other.
In a car, bevel gears change the direction of the driving force of the transmission shaft to the driving wheels.

bicycle   *noun*
A bicycle is a two-wheeled **vehicle**. The rider uses his or her feet to push the pedals around to provide energy. It is steered by moving the handlebars.
The children rode their bicycles to school every day.

bimetal thermostat ► **thermostat**

binary digit   *noun*
A binary digit is a number, either 0 or 1. **Computers** use binary digits, or **bits** for short, for counting and passing on information.
All the information in a computer is stored in binary digits.

binoculars ► page 21

bit ► **binary digit**

blast furnace   *noun*
A blast furnace is a kind of **furnace** used to take out, or extract, metal from metal ore. The ore is heated by an intense blast of air in the furnace, and oxygen and other **chemicals** are removed. The metal sinks to the bottom and is collected.
Iron is obtained from iron ore in a blast furnace.

block and tackle   *noun*
A block and tackle is a kind of **pulley** system used for lifting heavy weights. A length of rope or chain is wound two or more times between several pulleys and connected to the load to be lifted. The pulleys lessen the amount of effort needed.
We lifted the engine out of the boat with a block and tackle.

boat   *noun*
A boat is a small **ship**. Boats can be powered by oars, sails or **engines**.
There was a race between the two boats.

boiler   *noun*
1. A boiler is a **device** that uses **fuel** to boil water and make steam. The water runs through tubes above the firebox, which contains the burning fuel. The steam is then used in a **steam engine** or **steam turbine** to provide **power**.
A steam locomotive is driven by steam made in a boiler.

binoculars *noun*

Binoculars are a kind of **optical instrument** that make an object seem nearer. Binoculars contain **lenses** that increase, or magnify, the object's apparent size. The user looks through both eyepieces at the same time.
Through my binoculars I could see that the bird was a robin.

magnified image

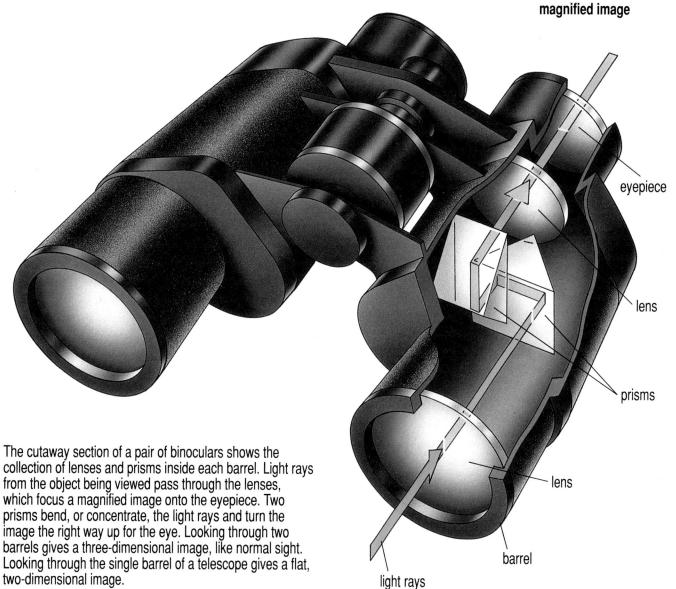

eyepiece

lens

prisms

lens

barrel

light rays

The cutaway section of a pair of binoculars shows the collection of lenses and prisms inside each barrel. Light rays from the object being viewed pass through the lenses, which focus a magnified image onto the eyepiece. Two prisms bend, or concentrate, the light rays and turn the image the right way up for the eye. Looking through two barrels gives a three-dimensional image, like normal sight. Looking through the single barrel of a telescope gives a flat, two-dimensional image.

bolt *noun*
A bolt is a kind of **simple machine** called a **screw**. It is a metal rod that fastens two things together. A spiral groove, called the thread, runs around the **shaft**, or shank, of the bolt. A **nut** twists onto this thread and can be pulled tight using a **wrench**. The thread of the nut fits together with the thread of the bolt.
A car engine is fixed tightly to the chassis with bolts.

bomb *noun*
A bomb is a **device** meant to explode or catch fire when it is dropped or thrown. Some bombs are dropped from **airplanes**, while fire bombs are sometimes used by terrorists to burn down buildings. Time bombs are connected to a timer and are designed to explode at a certain time.
All bombs are extremely dangerous.

boring machine ► **drill**

bottle opener *noun*
A bottle opener is a kind of **lever** that takes the top or lid off a bottle. One end of the bottle opener fits over the lid. Then it is levered off by raising the other end of the bottle opener.
Today, bottle openers are not as common as they used to be, because most bottles have screw-off caps.

bow-thruster *noun*
A bow-thruster is a **device** that helps some **ships** to **steer**. It has two **propellers** mounted on a **shaft** running across the bow of the ship under water.
The liner was able to dock smoothly with the help of its bow-thrusters.

box camera *noun*
A box camera is a kind of simple **camera** in the form of a box. It doesn't fold up and usually has a fixed focus and **shutter** speed.
The box camera took good pictures despite its simplicity.

brace and bit *noun*
A brace and bit is a tool for making holes in wood. The bit has a sharp spiral at one end. The other end is fixed in the brace. When the handle of the brace is turned, a **bevel gear** turns the bit and cuts away a circle of wood.
He made a round hole by using a brace and bit.

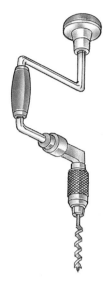

brake *noun*
A brake is a **device** for making a **machine**, such as an **automobile**, slow down or stop. It works by rubbing against a brake shoe or disc attached to the center of one or more **wheels**. This creates **friction** and causes the machine to lose energy.
The driver used the brake to stop at the traffic light.

breath tester ► **alcohol breath tester**

bubblejet printer *noun*
A bubblejet printer is a kind of **printing machine** used to print documents that have been typed on a **word processor**. The bubblejet printer shoots tiny drops of heated ink onto the paper.
After he had typed the letter, he used a bubblejet printer to print two copies.

bulb ► **light bulb**

bullet *noun*
A bullet is an explosive **device** that sends a small **missile** of metal or **plastic** from a hand gun or rifle. The **gun** explodes a charge in the body of the bullet, and this shoots the bullet head towards its target at enormous speed.
The rifleman loaded his gun with a bullet, aimed at the target, and fired.

burglar alarm *noun*

A burglar alarm is a **device** that gives a warning of unwanted intruders in a building. Some burglar alarms make bells or sirens ring. Others automatically send a message to the police. Modern burglar alarms have **sensors** that detect movement or body heat in a room.

The security guard heard the burglar alarm and went to see what was happening.

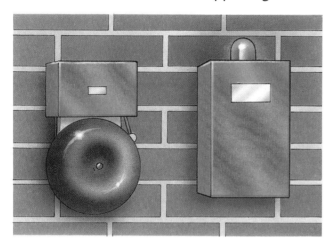

burner *noun*

A burner is the part of a heating or cooking **device** that gets hot.

She turned on the stove's burner and boiled some water.

butane *noun*

Butane is a colorless **gas**. It can be turned into a liquid by compressing it and can then be stored in a small container. Butane can be burned as a **fuel** by releasing the pressure through a **valve**, which allows it to become a gas once again.

We saw that the liquid butane was stored in steel cylinders.

byte *noun*

In **computer** science, a byte is eight **bits**. The size of a computer's memory is measured in bytes, **kilobytes** or **megabytes**. A kilobyte is 1,000 bytes and a megabyte is 1,000,000 bytes.

The computer had a memory of 640,000 bytes, or 640 kilobytes.

cable *noun*

A cable is a length of wires bundled together. Cables are usually made from **steel** or **copper**. Copper cables carry **electricity** and are often covered in **plastic**.

Cables bring electricity and telephone signals into our homes.

CAD ► **computer-aided design**

calculator *noun*

A calculator is a **machine** for counting quickly. It has number **keys** and function keys. When you press the number keys, information passes into the calculator. When you press the function keys, the calculator processes the information and the result is shown on the display panel.

If information is keyed in correctly, a calculator never makes a mistake.

calculate *verb*
calculation *noun*

cam *noun*

A cam is a kind of **wheel** that is not circular. It is used in **machines** to change circular movement into up and down movement.

Cams inside a car engine make the valves move up and down.

camera *noun*

A camera is a **device** for taking **photographs.** Light passes through **lenses** onto a piece of **film** coated with **chemicals** that are sensitive to light. When the film is processed, we can see the pictures.

I used my camera to take photographs of the football game.

camshaft *noun*
A camshaft is a **steel** rod with **cams** attached to it. As a camshaft spins, the cams raise and lower different parts of a **machine**.
The camshaft turned four cams in the engine.

can opener *noun*
A can opener is a **device** for cutting through the top of a can. Some can openers are simple **levers** with a sharp point at one end and a handle at the other. Others have a sharp-edged **wheel** that is moved by a **cog wheel**. A butterfly-shaped handle turns the cog wheel.
Some people have electric can openers fixed to the wall of their kitchen.

cantilever *noun*
A cantilever is a beam that is fixed at only one end. Cantilevers can be used to span a space where a support cannot be used.
The bridge had two cantilevers which stretched across the river.

cantilever spring *noun*
A cantilever spring is a thin, flat strip of metal fixed at one end. The other end is free to move. After it has moved, it springs back into its original position. For example, when you press the button of an **electric bell**, a cantilever spring connects an **electric circuit** and makes the bell ring.
Many electric gadgets contain a cantilever spring.

capacitor *noun*
A capacitor is a **device** for storing **electricity**. It has layers made up of thin sheets of metal that are separated by an **insulator**.
Capacitors are used in the electric circuits of radios, televisions, and computers.

capsule *noun*
A capsule is a closed compartment in a rocket that holds and protects people and instruments. It can be detached from the rest of the rocket.
The space capsule successfully splashed down.

capstan *noun*
A capstan is an upright drum on a ship, around which a rope is wound to pull up an anchor or lift weights.
The seamen hoisted the sail using the capstan.

car ► automobile

carburetor *noun*
A carburetor is part of a **gasoline engine** that mixes a fine spray of gasoline with air. Inside the engine, the mixture explodes and releases energy to turn the **motor**.
His car would not start because no gasoline was reaching the carburetor.

cargo liner *noun*
A cargo liner is a ship that carries mostly freight, or goods to be sold, over long distances.
The cargo liner transported cars from Europe to the United States.

cassette *noun*
A cassette is a **plastic** case containing recording **tape**. Audio cassettes record sound. Video cassettes can record sounds and pictures. The tape's magnetic surface is altered by **electric signals**.
I listened to a cassette recording of my favorite music.

cast iron *noun*

Cast iron is a kind of **iron** made by pouring molten iron into hollow molds. It is dark gray and breaks when dropped.
Some frying pans are made of cast iron.

catalytic converter *noun*

A catalytic converter is a **device** that is fitted to the **exhaust** system of a **vehicle** to cut down the amount of harmful **gases** released into the atmosphere. Catalytic converters contain metals that change the gases into less harmful ones.
Many countries have passed laws requiring all new cars to have a catalytic converter to reduce pollution.

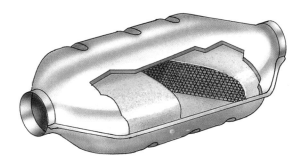

cathode-ray tube *noun*

A cathode-ray tube is a **glass** tube that forms pictures from **electronic signals**. An **electron gun** inside the tube fires **electrons** at a screen. This makes the screen glow, and a picture is built up from tiny points of light.
A television screen and a computer monitor are two examples of a cathode-ray tube.

CAT scanner *noun*

A CAT scanner is a **device** that produces **X-ray** images of any part of the body. It scans the object from different angles and produces a picture that doctors can study.
The doctor thought that the patient had serious heart disease and used a CAT scanner to find out.

central processing unit *noun*

A central processing unit, or CPU for short, is the part of a **computer** where the main work is done. It works on **data** that pass through it, using a **program**. The CPU then delivers the result to an **output**.
The central processing unit is the brain of a computer.

centrifugal force *noun*

Centrifugal force is a **force** that acts on objects when they turn, or revolve. Centrifugal force tries to fling objects away from their central point. The faster an object spins, the greater the centrifugal force.
The clothes in the dryer were pushed outward to the walls of the drum by centrifugal force.

centrifugal pump *noun*

A centrifugal pump is a **device** for separating liquids of different densities, such as **oil** and water. It spins the mixture, and the denser liquid, which is oil, is thrown to the sides.
Centrifugal pumps are used in dairies to separate milk from cream.

chain saw *noun*

A chain saw is a **machine** that is used for cutting wood. It has a chain of sharp-toothed links which is driven by a **gasoline engine** or an **electric motor**.
The lumberjack cut down the tree using a chain saw.

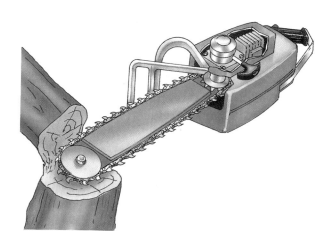

chassis *noun*
A chassis is the frame on which a machine is built. The machine's parts are all attached to the chassis.
The automobile engine is bolted firmly on to the chassis.

checkout ► **supermarket checkout**

chemical *noun*
A chemical is a single substance that is pure. All living and nonliving things are made of mixtures of chemicals.
Oxygen is a chemical in the air that we need to breathe to keep us alive.
chemical *adjective*

chimney *noun*
A chimney is a hollow pipe, usually made of brick or stone and connected to a fireplace, stove, or furnace. The chimney creates a flow of air from its base above the fire, toward its top. This flow of air brings oxygen to the fire and carries away the smoke and poisonous **gases** released by **combustion**.
The factory needed a tall chimney to draw enough air for the furnace.

chip ► **silicon chip**

chlorine *noun*
Chlorine is a yellow **gas** that dissolves in water. It is used in small quantities to make water safe to drink by killing harmful germs, such as bacteria. Chlorine has a strong smell, and is poisonous if swallowed.
They added chlorine to the water in the pool so it would be safe for swimming.

chromium *noun*
Chromium is a hard, silvery metal. It does not corrode. Chromium is often used to plate other metals, giving them a long-lasting, shiny finish. Chromium is mixed with **iron** to make stainless **steel**. Such a mixture of metals is called an **alloy**.
Many knives and forks are made from steel that contains chromium.

circuit *noun*
A circuit is a closed path through which **electricity** flows. If the wires forming the circuit are separated, the circuit is broken and the flow of electricity is halted.
She used a battery to provide power to the circuit.

circuit board *noun*
A circuit board is a **device** that is part of an **electronic appliance**. It is a sheet of **plastic** covered with thin **copper** strips, which join together its parts, or components. A circuit board is sometimes called a printed circuit.
The technician repaired the computer by installing a new circuit board.

circuit breaker *noun*
A circuit breaker is a kind of switch in an **electric circuit**. It automatically switches off the **electricity** if too much current flows into the circuit or if too many appliances are plugged in at one time, causing an overload. Circuit breakers can be used instead of fuses. You can reset a circuit breaker by putting the switch on again.
The circuit breaker cut off the electric current and all the lights went out.

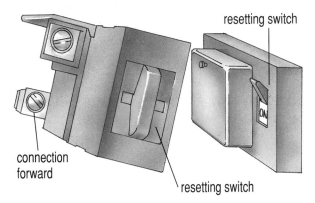
resetting switch
connection forward
resetting switch

circular saw *noun*
A circular saw is a kind of **machine** for cutting wood or other materials. Its blade is like a **wheel**, with sharp teeth around the edge. A circular saw is powered by an **electric motor**. The saw is sometimes fixed on a table, half above and half below the surface.
He cut the wood with a circular saw.

cistern *noun*
A cistern is a **tank** used to store water. Rainwater is collected in the cistern, which is usually located underground, and used for drinking, washing clothes, watering gardens, and other household uses.
Cisterns are sometimes used where there are no water pipes or wells.

clamp *noun*
A clamp is a **tool** that holds things together so that work can be done on them. Some clamps work by tightening a **screw** or **bolt**. Others work by pressing a **lever**.
The clamp held the two pieces of wood together while the glue set.
clamp verb

clock *noun*
A clock is a **machine** for telling the time. Clocks can work either **mechanically** or **electronically**. Large mechanical clocks, such as **pendulum clocks**, are often driven by a weight. Smaller mechanical clocks are driven by small **springs** called mainsprings. An **analogue** clock has hands that move around a **dial**. A **digital** clock shows the time in numerals.
Digital clocks are usually electronic.

clockwork motor *noun*
A clockwork motor is a kind of **machine**. It stores energy in a circular **spring**, which is wound up with a **key**. This energy is used to turn **gear wheels**. Clockwork motors are often used in simple toys.
The clock is driven by a clockwork motor.

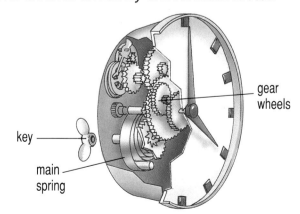

gear wheels

key

main spring

clutch *noun*
A clutch is a part of a **vehicle** that is found between the **engine** and the **gearbox**. It has a rotating plate fixed to the engine and a similar one fixed to the gearbox **shaft**. Normally, they are pressed together by **springs**. A driver who wants to change gear presses a pedal to depress the clutch. This disconnects the engine from the gearbox. After the gear has been changed, the clutch is connected, or engaged, again.
He depressed the clutch pedal and shifted into top gear.

coal *noun*
Coal is a black, solid fossil formed from the remains of plants that died millions of years ago. Coal is mined underground, where it is found in layers, or seams. It is used in many parts of the world in **power stations** to produce **steam** for **turbines**, and for cooking and heating in homes. The two most important types of coal are hard coal, or anthracite, and soft, or bituminous, coal.
Coal was the fuel that was burned in steam locomotives.

coal face cutter ► page 28

coal gas *noun*
Coal gas is formed when **coal** is heated in a closed space with no air. It is a mixture of **gases**, some of which are poisonous.
Coal gas was used for lighting and heating.

coal tar *noun*
Coal tar is a thick, black liquid formed when **coal** is burned and changes into **coke**. Coal tar contains many useful **chemicals**.
Coal tar is used in some disinfectants.

cobalt *noun*
Cobalt is a very hard and silvery metal. It is mixed with **iron** to make cobalt **steel**. This is used in the manufacture of hard cutting **tools** and **drills**.
The cobalt is mixed with molten iron inside the furnace.

coal face cutter   *noun*

A coal face cutter is a **machine** for cutting **coal** in a mine. Some cutters shear off slices of coal and throw them onto a **conveyor** belt. Others are like huge **drills** which work along the side of the coal face.

A modern coal face cutter can produce 900 tons of coal per hour.

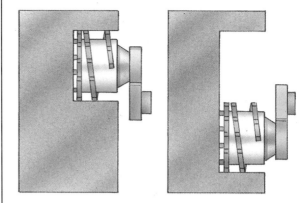

The cutting head of a coal face cutter can be adjusted to cope with high or low layers, or seams, of coal.

cockpit *noun*
The cockpit of an **airplane** is where the pilot sits. It contains the instruments and controls. The cockpit of a large airplane is called the **flight deck**.
The pilot climbed into the cockpit and strapped himself in.

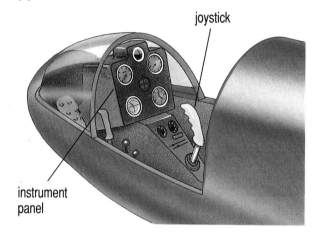

joystick

instrument panel

code *noun*
A code is a special language made up of signals, symbols, letters, or numbers. The purpose of a code is to keep a message short or secret. In computers, codes are used as a method of storing or sending information. The binary code is the system of **binary digits** used by computers. A number code is used to open a **combination lock**.
All information stored in computers is in code form.

coffee grinder *noun*
A coffee grinder chops coffee beans and turns them into ground coffee. It has a sharp blade that spins around inside a container. Most coffee grinders have **electric motors**. Some are operated by hand.
He put some beans in the coffee grinder to make fresh coffee for breakfast.

cog *noun*
A cog is a metal tooth on the outside edge of a **gear wheel**. The cogs on one gear fit, or mesh, together with the cogs on another.
The gear had 20 cogs around its outside edge.

cog wheel *noun*
A cog wheel is a wheel with **cogs** around its outside edge. The cogs on one cog wheel usually connect with the cogs on another. In a **watch** with an **anchor escapement**, the teeth of the escapement connect with a cog wheel.
Cog wheels transfer energy from one part of a machine to another.

coil *noun*
1. A coil is a shape made when a length of wire, rope, or similar material is wound many times in a circle.
The sailors made coils of rope on the deck of the ship.
2. Part of an **electric circuit**, a coil is a length of **copper** wire wound around an **iron** core. When **electric current** flows into it, the coil becomes an **electromagnet**.
Electric signals passing into the coil of a loudspeaker make the loudspeaker vibrate and produce sound.

coil spring *noun*
A coil spring is a length of metal wire formed into a **coil**. If the coil is squeezed together or pulled apart, it will return to its original shape once the **force** is removed. Coil springs are sometimes called helical springs.
There are coil springs inside the seat on a bicycle.

coke *noun*
Coke is a kind of **coal** from which most of the **gases** have been removed. It is used in **blast furnaces** to make **iron**.
Coke gives off very strong heat.

combination lock *noun*
A combination lock is a **lock** that does not need a **key**. It opens when a set of **wheels** are turned so that they show a number. This number is a **code** that is known only to the owner of the **device** to which the lock is fitted.
Only the manager knew the number that would open the safe's combination lock.

combine harvester ► page 32

combust *verb*
Combust means to burn. When something combusts, it combines with oxygen and gives off heat energy.
Ash is the waste product left behind when wood combusts.
combustion *noun*

combustion chamber *noun*
A combustion chamber is the sealed part of a **furnace** where burning, or **combustion**, takes place.
Iron ore, limestone, and coke were loaded into the combustion chamber of the furnace.

command *noun*
A command is an instruction to do something. Commands can be given to a **computer** by using a **keyboard**, a **mouse**, or a **joystick**.
She gave the command to her computer to print her poem.
command *verb*

communications *plural noun*
Communications are ways of sending messages between living things or between **machines**. When we talk or write to someone, we are using communications. **Telecommunications** are communications using **electronics**.
The telephone allows communication over a long distance.

commutator *noun*
A commutator is a part of some **electric motors** and **generators**. When it revolves inside the fixed part of the **machine**, an **electric current** is generated.
The commutator spins around inside the electric motor.

compact disk *noun*
A compact disk is a thin, **plastic disk** that contains **digital** information. It is often used for music recordings, but can also carry other kinds of information.
For her birthday, she received a compact disk of her favorite singer.

compass *noun*
A compass is an instrument that shows the direction in which someone or something is traveling. A **magnetic compass** contains a magnet in the shape of a needle. The ends of the needle always point to magnetic north and south.
The sailors used a compass to find their way north.

compressed air *noun*
Compressed air is air that has been squeezed into a small space. This increases its pressure. When compressed air is released, it returns to normal atmospheric pressure with **force**. This force can be used as a source of energy.
In an auto factory, car bodies are sprayed with paint by using compressed air.

compressor *noun*
A compressor is a **machine** for squeezing air or other **gases** into a small space. It is powered by a **motor** using **electricity**, **oil**, or **gasoline**.
The workers used jackhammers powered by a compressor.
compress *verb*

computer *noun*
A computer is an **electronic machine** that can assess information very quickly. Information is given to the computer through an **input**. When the computer has finished the task, it presents the results on an **output**. This is usually a **visual display unit**, or a printout.
He used his computer every day at the office.

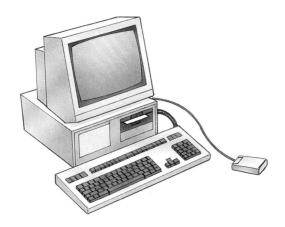

computer-aided design *noun*
Computer-aided design, or CAD for short, is a way of designing objects with the help of a **computer**. The designer can see on a computer **screen** how an object will look and behave when it is built.
Computer-aided design is used to design cars, ships, buildings, and machines.

concave lens *noun*
A concave lens is a piece of ground **glass** thicker at the edges than in the middle. Concave lenses make rays of light spread out. They are used in **movie projectors**.
He used a slide projector with a concave lens to shine the picture on the wall.

concrete mixer *noun*
A concrete mixer is a **machine** that mixes sand, gravel, water, and cement together in a revolving drum that is driven by a **motor**. Concrete is used for construction.
The builders used a concrete mixer to make concrete for the sidewalk.

condenser *noun*
1. A condenser is a **device** for storing **electricity**. It is often called a **capacitor**.
The condenser on the car's engine releases a spark to ignite the fuel.
2. A condenser is part of the equipment used to change a **gas** into a liquid.
The condenser cools the gas to convert it to a liquid.

control panel *noun*
A control panel is a display of instruments that shows how a **machine** is performing. The instruments show such things as the machine's speed and temperature.
The control panel of a car is called the dashboard.

control surfaces *plural noun*
Control surfaces are parts of an **aircraft** that can be made to move by the pilot to control the direction of the plane. The **ailerons** along the trailing edge of the wings, tilt the aircraft left or right. The **rudder** on top of the tail plane turns the aircraft left or right. The elevators at the base of the tail plane make the aircraft climb or dive.
The pilot turned the aircraft by moving the control surfaces.

control tower ► page 34

control unit *noun*
A control unit is a **device** that is part of a **machine**. The operator of the machine presses buttons or moves **levers** on the control unit to make the machine perform a task.
Pressing buttons on an elevator's control unit makes the elevator go up or down.

combine harvester *noun*

A combine harvester is a large farm
machine that cuts cereal crops, separates
the grain, and throws out the stalks and
husks.

*Using a combine harvester, the farmer was
able to finish the harvest in one day.*

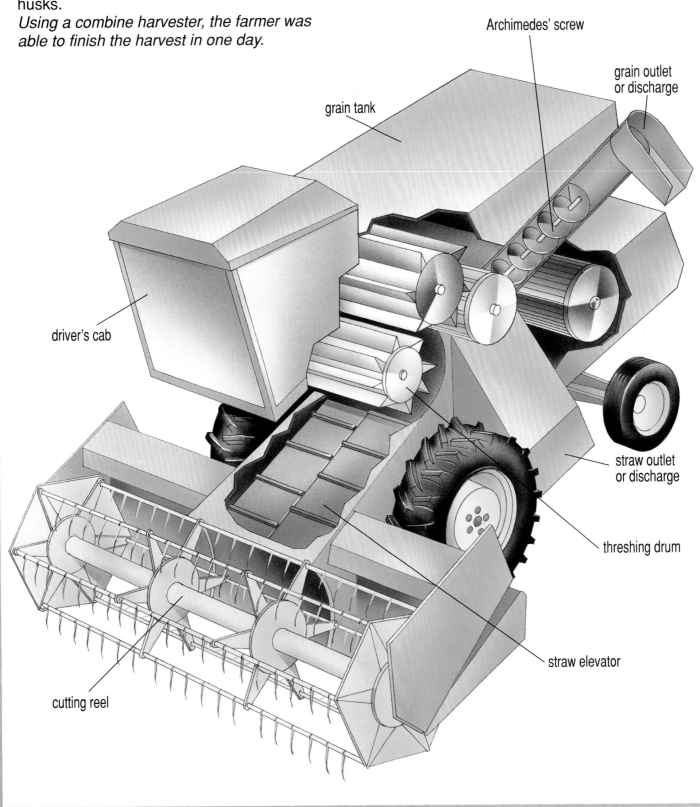

Archimedes' screw

grain outlet
or discharge

grain tank

driver's cab

straw outlet
or discharge

threshing drum

cutting reel

straw elevator

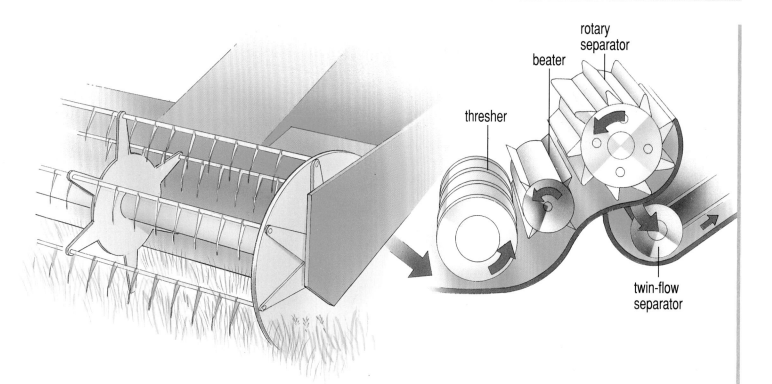

The height of a combine harvester's cutting reel can be changed to cut crops of different lengths.

The crop is threshed and the grain separated in four stages, using four different kinds of drum or rotor.

The separated grain flows through the discharge pipe into a container called a grain pot. An Archimedes' screw inside the pipe keeps the grain flowing.

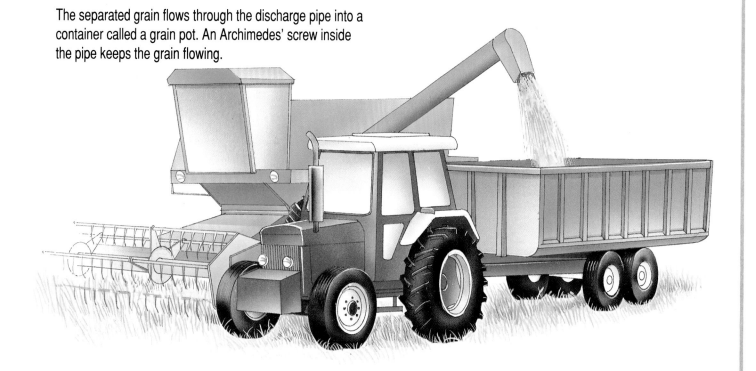

control tower   *noun*

A control tower is a tall building at an airport.
People called air traffic controllers give radio
instructions to pilots, telling them when it is
safe to taxi, take off, or land their **aircraft**.
*There is a good view of the runways from
the airport control tower.*

convex lens   *noun*
A convex lens is a piece of ground **glass** thick in the middle and thin at the edges. A convex lens concentrates light passing through it onto a focal point.
There are convex lenses in cameras and binoculars.

conveyor   *noun*
A conveyor is a **machine** that carries things automatically from one place to another. It has a moving belt made of **steel**, rubber, or **plastic**. Conveyors carry machine parts in assembly plants, luggage at airports, and **coal** in mines.
The parts of the engine were bolted on as it traveled along on the conveyor.

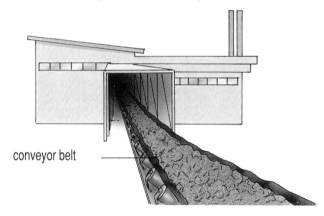

conveyor belt

coolant   *noun*
A coolant is a liquid used to take away excess heat in a **machine**. The heat produced by an **engine** is drawn off through pipes close to the moving parts. When metal is being cut or shaped on a **lathe**, a special **oil**-and-water mixture is sprayed on the cutting tool to stop it from becoming too hot.
Water is used as a coolant in most car engines.

cooling system   *noun*
A cooling system is part of an **engine**. It is made up of a **pump** that supplies a **coolant** through pipes close to the engine's working parts to cool them.
The car engine overheated because there was a fault in the cooling system.

cooling tower   *noun*
A cooling tower is part of a **nuclear power station**. It is made of concrete. Hot water from the **turbines** sprays down inside the cooling tower, where the cold air cools the water. Some water is given off as vapor from the top of the tower.
We were a long way away from the power station, but we could see its cooling towers in the distance.

copper   *noun*
Copper is a **chemical** element. It is a soft, reddish-brown metal. A very good conductor of heat and **electricity**, copper is used to make pipes and electric wires. When copper is mixed with other metals, it forms **alloys**, such as bronze and brass.
The electrical circuits in a house are made of copper wire covered with plastic.

counterweight   *noun*
A counterweight is a weight used to **balance** a moving part in a **machine** so that its movement can be easily controlled. The counterweights in a window make it easier to raise or lower the sash.
The function of the counterweight in an elevator shaft is to balance the weight of the elevator.

CPU ► **central processing unit**

crane   *noun*
A crane is a **machine** for lifting and moving heavy loads. Some cranes are fixed to the ground. Others move along rails, hang from **gantries**, or are mounted on **vehicles**.
The crane lifted the boulder onto the back of the truck.

crank   *noun*
A crank is a part of a **machine**. It is a **shaft** bent at right angles. A crank changes to-and-fro motion into circular motion.
The crank of a bicycle turns the up-and-down movement of the knees into circular motion.

crankshaft *noun*
A crankshaft is part of an **internal combustion engine**. It is a thick, steel rod bent at right angles, to which the **pistons** are connected. When the pistons move up and down, the crankshaft turns, or revolves.
The starter motor turned the crankshaft to start the car's engine.

crop duster *noun*
A crop duster is a small **airplane** or a **helicopter** used to spray fertilizer or pesticide onto fields where crops are being grown.
The crop duster was unable to fertilize the fields because it was too windy.

crop sprayer *noun*
A crop sprayer is a **device** for spraying water, fertilizers, or pesticides onto growing farm crops. It has a tank containing liquid, a **pump**, and a nozzle that makes a fine spray. Crop sprayers are hand-held, pulled by a **tractor**, or attached to small **aircraft**.
The farmer used a crop sprayer to kill the aphids that had attacked his beans.

crude oil ► petroleum

cutoff *noun*
A cutoff is a **device** that automatically cuts off **electricity** or the fuel supply to a **machine**. It works if there is an emergency or if the machine has broken down. Some cutoffs work **electronically** to operate switches. Others work by **springs** and wires.
When the engine became too hot, the cutoff shut it down.

cutting machine *noun*
A cutting machine is a **device** for cutting and shaping metal. It is fitted with sharp cutting **tools**. Some cutting machines cut across the metal. Others cut it from above.
The mechanic shaped a new cover for the engine, using a cutting machine.

cylinder *noun*
A cylinder is part of a **machine**. It is a hollow tube with a **piston** that moves up and down inside it. Pressure placed inside the cylinder makes the piston move.
Many cars have four-cylinder engines.
cylindrical *adjective*

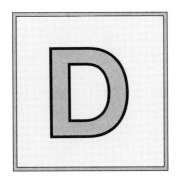

dairy machines ► page 38

daisy-wheel printer *noun*
A daisy-wheel printer is a **device** that is used with a **computer** to produce a printed **output**.
Each spoke of a daisy-wheel printer's wheel carries a different print character.

dashboard *noun*
A dashboard is a part of the inside of an automobile, in front of the driver.
The dashboard has instruments that show the car's speed, the amount of fuel left, and other information.

data *plural noun*
Data is a plural word that means information. **Computers** receive data from a **disk**, **magnetic tape**, or other **input**. They then store the data and process it.
People and computers use data to solve problems and answer questions.

database *noun*
A database is a collection of information. It can be stored on a **disk** or on **magnetic tape**, or in the **memory** of a **computer**. The computer can find each piece of information very quickly.
The club stored the names and addresses of all its members on a database.

deflector *noun*
A deflector is a part of a **machine** that changes the direction of material striking it.
Deflectors are often used to separate waste material.

derailleur gear *noun*
A derailleur gear is a set of **gears** on a **bicycle**. It is used to make the most of the **power** delivered to a bicycle's rear **wheel** by the cyclist. A derailleur gear has a number of **gear wheels** that are brought into action by moving a control **lever**.
Her bicycle had derailleur gears, and so she was able to reach the top of the hill first.

derrick *noun*
A derrick is a kind of **crane**. It raises or lowers an object above a fixed point.
Derricks are used on oil exploration rigs to drill for oil.

desalination *noun*
Desalination is the removal of salt from sea water. Equipment for doing this is called a desalination plant. There are a number of different ways of desalinating salt water.
Water that has been desalinated is suitable for drinking.
desalinate *verb*

detector ► **sensors and detectors**

device *noun*
A device is a small, manufactured object that is designed for a special purpose. **Locks**, switches, and lamps are all different kinds of devices.
A meter is a device for showing measurements.

dairy machines *noun*

Dairy machines are pieces of equipment that treat, or process, cow's milk. Some **machines** milk the cows. Some machines heat the milk to make it safe. Other machines remove the cream to make skimmed milk. Others put the milk into bottles or cartons and seal them.

Milk from the farm is processed in dairy machines.

A dairy

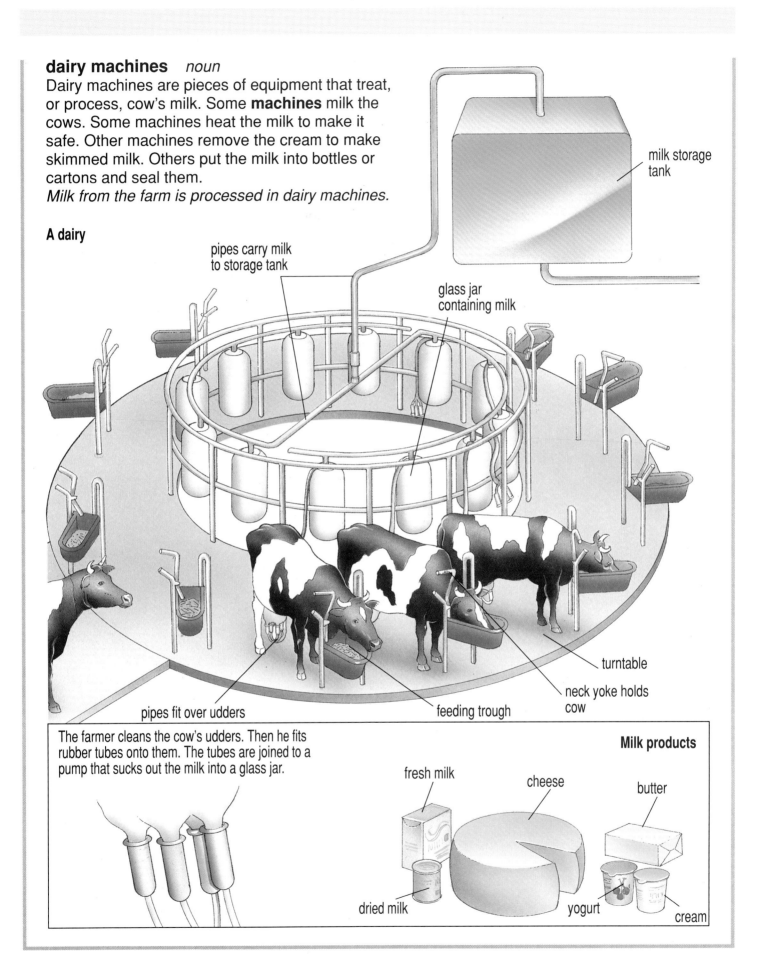

milk storage tank

pipes carry milk to storage tank

glass jar containing milk

turntable

neck yoke holds cow

feeding trough

pipes fit over udders

The farmer cleans the cow's udders. Then he fits rubber tubes onto them. The tubes are joined to a pump that sucks out the milk into a glass jar.

Milk products

fresh milk

cheese

butter

dried milk

yogurt

cream

dial *noun*
A dial is a **device** that is used on many measuring instruments. It usually has a round face like a **clock**.
A hand, or needle, on a dial points to measurements marked around the outside.

diaphragm *noun*
A diaphragm is a thin, flat sheet of metal, rubber, or **plastic**. When a **force** pushes against a diaphragm, it moves. In a **loudspeaker**, a diaphragm changes **electrical signals** into sounds as it vibrates.
A diaphragm in a telephone changes signals coming through the wire into sounds.

diaphragm pump *noun*
A diaphragm pump is a **device** for pumping **gases** or liquids. It uses a **diaphragm** to make a **vacuum**. The gas or liquid is drawn into the pump by the vacuum and then pushed out, or expelled, when the diaphragm moves in the opposite direction. A **diaphragm valve** keeps the flow moving in the right direction.
A bicycle pump is an example of a diaphragm pump.

diaphragm valve *noun*
A diaphragm valve is a **device** that allows a liquid or **gas** to pass in only one direction. The diaphragm fits loosely across an opening to allow the liquid or gas to pass, but closes tightly to stop it from escaping.
The human heart has a type of diaphragm valve to keep the blood flowing.

die-casting *noun*
Die-casting is a way of forming metal. The metal is heated until it is molten. Then it is poured into a mold called a die. Die-casting is used to produce rough articles that must be finished by hand or **machine** before use. The dies can be used again and again.
Die-casting allowed the workers to produce hundreds of model soldiers in a day.

diesel engine *noun*
A diesel engine is a kind of **internal combustion engine**. It burns a mixture of air and **diesel fuel** to produce energy. The mixture is ignited by the heat produced by compression, rather than by a **spark plug**. The diesel engine was patented by a German inventor, Rudolf Diesel. Another name for a diesel engine is a compression ignition engine.
Diesel engines are often used to generate electricity at a fairground.

diesel fuel *noun*
Diesel fuel is a liquid made from **oil**. It is used as a fuel for **diesel engines**. Another name for diesel fuel is DERV, which is short for Diesel Engine Road Vehicle.
He filled the truck's tanks with diesel fuel.

differential *noun*
A differential is a system of **gears** that allows parts of a **machine** to move at different speeds. The differential in an **automobile** lets the driving **wheels** move at different speeds when rounding corners.
The differential allows the outside wheel to travel faster than the inside wheel.

digger *noun*
A digger is a large **machine** for making holes and trenches in the ground. It is a kind of **tractor** that digs a shovel-shaped **tool** into the ground. The digging arm is powered by **hydraulics**.
The gang used a digger to make a trench for the new water pipes.

digital *adjective*
Digital describes the use of numbers for any purpose. A digital **watch** shows the time in numbers. An **analogue** watch shows the time by hands that move around a **dial**.
The numbers 0 and 1 are numbers that digital computers use to store data.
digit *noun*

digital audio tape *noun*
Digital audio tape, or DAT for short, is **magnetic tape** that contains recorded **electric signals**. These can be fed into a **digital** player and changed back into sound signals. Recordings made on digital audio tape are of a very high quality.
She gave her brother a new stereo that used digital audio tape.

digital clock *noun*
A digital clock shows the time in digits instead of by hands moving around a dial. Digital clocks are usually powered by electricity.
The time on his digital clock was 12:30 p.m.

direct current *noun*
Direct current, or DC for short, is a kind of **electric current** that flows through a **circuit** in only one direction. **Batteries** send direct current to the **devices** for which they provide **power**. The opposite of direct current is **alternating current**.
A battery produces direct current for a flashlight.

disc brakes *noun*
Disc brakes are used to slow down or stop a **machine**. A disc is attached to the machine's moving parts. Pads push against the disc to stop the machine by creating **friction**. In an **automobile** disc brakes are attached to the **hub** of the **wheel** to slow them down.
She applied the disc brakes and brought the car to a stop.

disc drive ► **disk drive**

dish antenna *noun*
A dish antenna is a kind of **aerial** that is curved like a dish. It collects radio signals and passes them to a **receiver**. Dish antennae that are made to receive radio signals from the stars may be up to 1,000 feet across.
The dish antenna on the side of our house allows us to receive television programs via satellite.

dishwasher *noun*
A dishwasher is an electrical **appliance** that cleans dirty plates, glasses, and cutlery. It rinses, washes, and then dries them. A dishwasher is powered by an **electric motor**.
After the party, we put all the dirty dishes into the dishwasher.

disk ► **floppy disk, hard disk**

disk *noun*
A disk is a round, thin, flat object. A **compact disk** is a kind of disk used to record and play back sound.
He put a compact disk into the disk player and they listened to the music.

disk drive *noun*
A disk drive is part of a **computer** that collects **data** from the **hard** or the **floppy disks** and passes it to the **central processing unit**, or vice versa.
He put a floppy disk into the computer's disk drive.

dot matrix printer   *noun*
A dot matrix printer is a **device** that is often used for the **output** of a **computer**. It has a **print head** that contains a number of needles, which print characters by making ink dots on the paper.
She used a dot matrix printer to print the work she had done on her computer.

dredger   *noun*
A dredger is a kind of **ship** that clears mud and sand from the beds of harbors so that they are deep enough for other ships to use. The mud is collected by a chain of large shovels and then taken away to be dumped.
The dredger was hard at work because the storm had made a sandbank in the harbor.

drill   *noun*
A drill is a **tool** for making holes. The part of the drill that cuts the hole is made from **steel** and is called the bit. It has two special grooves cut into it that make it look like a large **screw**. The edges of the grooves are very sharp. Drills are used by carpenters, metalworkers, road builders, and workers on **oil rigs**.
He drilled holes in the metal.
drill   *verb*

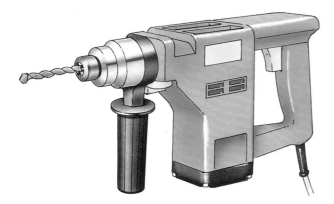

drive ► disk drive

drive cog   *noun*
A drive cog is part of a **machine**. It is the **gear** that turns the working parts of the machine.
The drive cog turned the shaft.

drive shaft   *noun*
A drive shaft is a **steel** rod that sends, or transmits, **power** from the **engine** to the moving parts of a **machine**.
The car's drive shaft connected with the gears of the rear axle and made it turn.

driving gears   *noun*
Driving gears are a set of **gears** that make the most of the **power** delivered to a **vehicle**'s **wheels** by the **engine**.
Most cars have four or five driving gears.

drop hammer   *noun*
A drop hammer is a large **tool** used in an **iron foundry**. It has a heavy head that is dropped onto red-hot iron to beat it into shape.
The men wore earmuffs to protect their ears from the noise of the drop hammer as it pounded the iron.

drum brake   *noun*
A drum brake is a **device** for slowing down or stopping a **vehicle** or **machine**. A **steel** drum is fixed to the **hubs** of the **wheels** and revolves with it. Pads, or shoes, push out against the inside of the drum to cause **friction** and slow it down.
Most older cars have drum brakes, but most newer cars have disk brakes.

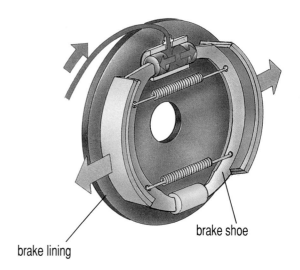

brake lining

brake shoe

dynamometer *noun*
A dynamometer is an instrument for measuring energy. It is used to test how well a **machine** works.
The engineers tested the power of the new engine with a dynamometer.

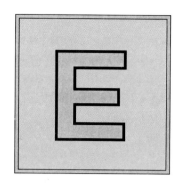

earphones *plural noun*
Earphones are an electrical **device** that allows one person to listen to sounds without disturbing other people. They fit inside the ear and work just like a telephone **receiver**.
My brother was doing his homework and needed quiet, so I listened to records on my earphones.

earth drill *noun*
An earth drill is a **tool** for making holes in the ground. Some earth drills are shaped like a flat-bladed corkscrew and are small enough for one or two men to turn by hand. Other earth drills are **power** operated and may be as large as a train. These very large earth drills are used for tunneling. They have many rotating cutting blades.
They dug for oil with an earth drill.

egg whisk ► **whisk**

electric bell *noun*
An electric bell is a **device** that gives a warning. When the button is pressed, an **electric current** and a magnet make a small **hammer** vibrate against the metal bell case. This makes a ringing sound.
They rang the electric bell during the fire drill.

electric cable *noun*
An electric cable is a bundle of long wires that carry **electric current**. The wires are usually made of **copper** and covered with **plastic** to **insulate** the cable.
They dug a trench to take the electric cable to the new house.

electric circuit   *noun*

An electric circuit is a closed pathway along which **electric current** flows. It is usually made of wires, which link the source of **electricity** to **appliances**. Most electric circuits have switches so that they can be turned on or off.
When she flipped the light switch, the electric circuit was completed.

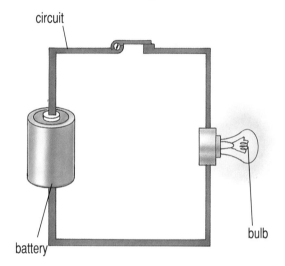

circuit
battery
bulb

electric current   *noun*

An electric current is a flow of **electricity**. It is created when **electrons** flow through an **electric circuit**. An electric current can be **alternating** or **direct**.
The on-off switch controls the flow of electric current through a radio.

electric drill   *noun*

An electric drill is a **tool** for making holes. It is powered by an **electric motor**. Dentists use small electric drills to remove tooth decay.
He used an electric drill to make a hole in the wall.

electric generator   *noun*

An electric generator is a **machine** that makes **electricity**. It uses **coal**, water, **oil**, or **nuclear** material as **fuel**. A generator can produce either **direct current** or **alternating current**.
Electric generators are found at power stations.

electric guitar   *noun*

An electric guitar is a musical instrument that is played by plucking the strings. It is connected to an **amplifier**, which makes it sound louder.
Two of the musicians in the group played electric guitars.

electricity   *noun*

Electricity is a kind of energy. It can be produced by **batteries** or in a **power station**. Electricity is used to light lamps and power electric **tools** and **appliances**.
Electricity also occurs naturally as lightning in thunder storms.

electric mixer   *noun*

An electric mixer is an **appliance** used in cooking. It contains an **electric motor** that turns a blade or **whisk**, which mixes up the ingredients of the dish that is being prepared.
She used the electric mixer to combine the flour and margarine.

electric motor   ▶ page 44

electric signal   *noun*

An electric signal is a kind of message produced by **electricity**. Electric signals flow through a **television** set when it is switched on, allowing us to see the picture and hear the sound.
The loudspeaker changes electric signals into sound waves.

electric motor   *noun*

An electric motor is a **device** that changes electrical energy into **kinetic energy**. It uses an **electric current** to turn a **drive shaft**.
The electric motor in a vacuum cleaner turns a fan that sucks up dust.

Electric trains, such as the French TGV, are powered by electric motors. Electricity is picked up by the motor from an overhead cable or from a third rail running beside the usual pair of rails.

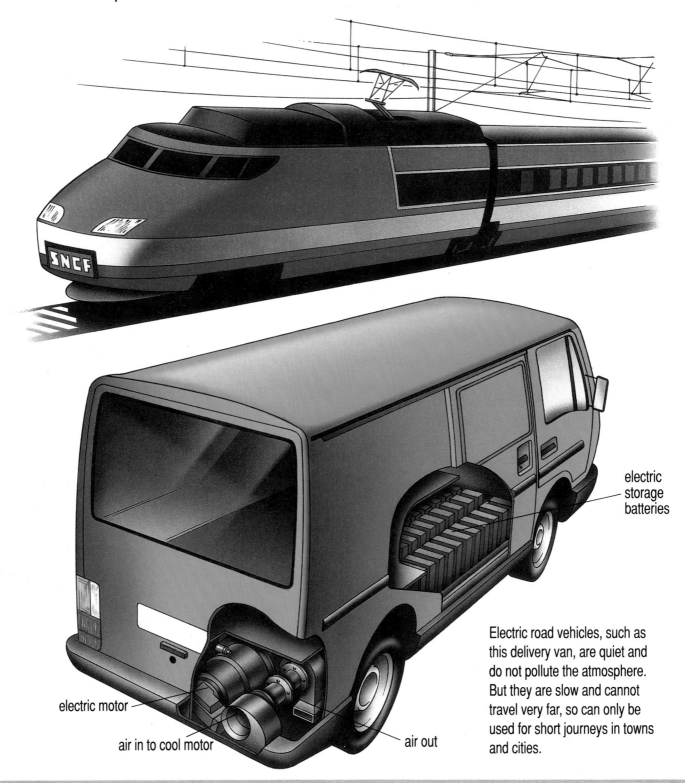

electric storage batteries

electric motor

air in to cool motor

air out

Electric road vehicles, such as this delivery van, are quiet and do not pollute the atmosphere. But they are slow and cannot travel very far, so can only be used for short journeys in towns and cities.

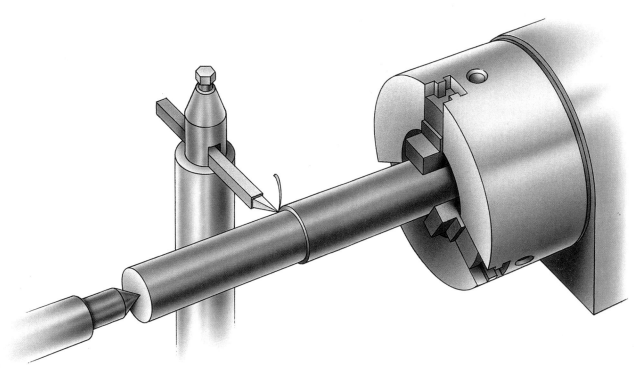

Electric motors are used to drive many kinds of machine tool, such as this lathe.

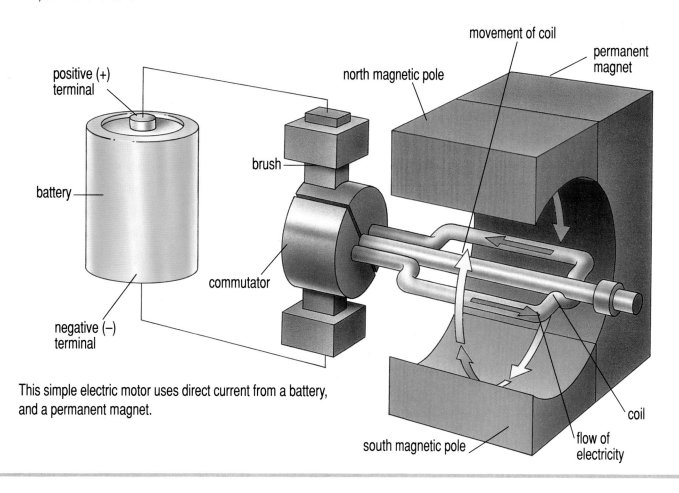

positive (+) terminal

movement of coil

permanent magnet

north magnetic pole

brush

battery

commutator

negative (−) terminal

This simple electric motor uses direct current from a battery, and a permanent magnet.

coil

flow of electricity

south magnetic pole

electrocardiograph   *noun*
An electrocardiograph is an instrument that records the action of a person's heartbeat. An electrical impulse is produced each time the heart beats.
The patient's irregular heartbeat was picked up by the cardiograph.

electrode   *noun*
An electrode is part of an electric **battery**. Each battery has two electrodes. **Electric current** flows from the positive electrode into a **circuit** and returns to the negative electrode. On the outside of a battery, the positive electrode is marked with a plus sign and the negative electrode with a minus sign.
It is important to put a battery into a flashlight with the electrodes facing the right way.

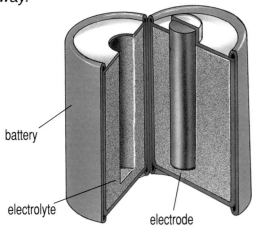

battery
electrolyte
electrode

electrolysis   *noun*
Electrolysis is a process in which **electricity** causes **chemical** changes. When electricity flows through certain liquids, it causes new substances to form.
Chlorine gas is produced by electrolysis.

electromagnet   *noun*
An electromagnet is a **coil** of wire wound around an **iron** rod. When an **electric current** passes through the wire, the rod becomes magnetic.
Many electrical appliances contain electromagnets.

electron   *noun*
An electron is a tiny particle of negatively charged matter. There are electrons in all the atoms in the universe.
An electric current is made up of moving electrons.

electron gun   *noun*
An electron gun is part of a **television receiver**. It uses **electricity** to fire a stream of **electrons** at a screen. The electrons move very quickly and create the picture seen on the screen.
The electron gun is at the back of the television set.

electronic   *adjective*
Electronic describes **devices** that use streams of **electrons** to make them work. **Radios**, **televisions**, and **computers** are all electronic devices.
Television engineers study electronic engineering as part of their training.
electronics   *noun*

electron microscope

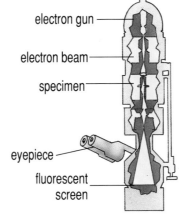

electron gun
electron beam
specimen
eyepiece
fluorescent screen

virus magnified 190,000 times by electron microscope

electron microscope   *noun*
An electron microscope is an instrument that makes very small objects look larger, or magnifies them. It contains an **electron gun**, which is aimed at the object to be magnified. The image is shown on a screen.
An electron microscope can magnify objects up to one million times.

electronic engineering *noun*
Electronic engineering is the part of electrical engineering that is concerned with electronics and the use of electronic devices in various machines such as **radios**, **televisions**, **computers**, and others.
Because they were interested in television, they took a course in electronic engineering.

electronic flash *noun*
An electronic flash is a **device** on some **cameras**. It operates a flash bulb, which lights up when a **photograph** is taken. An electronic flash is needed when there is not enough natural light. It is **powered** by a **battery**.
The photographer uses an electronic flash when taking pictures at night.

electronic signal ► **electric signal**

electroplating *noun*
Electroplating is a process that coats one metal with a thin layer of another metal. The metals are put into a solution that carries an **electric current**, which causes a thin layer of one metal to form on the other.
Chromium is an expensive but tough metal. It is used to electroplate the surface of cheaper metal, such as **iron**, so it won't rust.
Electroplating is used to make silver-plated tableware.
electroplate *verb*

electrostatic painting *noun*
Electrostatic painting is a process used to paint **automobile** bodies. The car body and a spray gun are given different electric charges. The paint completes an **electric circuit** as it is sprayed onto the metal.
Electrostatic painting gives a car body an even coat of paint.

electrostatic precipitator *noun*
An electrostatic precipitator is a **machine** that removes solid particles from smoke. It passes the smoke through a **network** of wires that carry an **electric current**. The solid particles become electrically charged and are attracted onto collecting plates.
An electrostatic precipitator helps to cut down pollution that is caused by factory smoke.

enameling *noun*
Enameling is a process that covers metal with a hard, glasslike coating. It is used for decoration and to protect metal from corrosion. The metal surface of the object is covered with a wet powder of enamel. It is then heated to a very high temperature so that the enamel melts and sticks, to the surface of the metal.
Enameling protected the instrument case from the weather.

endoscope *noun*
An endoscope is an instrument for viewing the internal parts of the body. It contains a tiny **television camera** that can be placed inside the body through a tube.
The doctor used an endoscope to examine the patient's stomach.
endoscopy *noun*

engine *noun*
An engine is a **machine** that uses energy from **fuel** to perform tasks. **Steam engines** and **internal combustion engines** are two kinds of engine.
The car that won the race had a very powerful engine.

epicyclic gears *noun*
Epicyclic gears are parts of some **machines**. They consist of two **gear wheels**, one small and the other larger. The smaller gear fits into the larger and turns around inside it. Larger gears turn more slowly than smaller ones.
Some cars have epicyclic gears.

epoxy *adjective or noun*
Epoxy refers to something that contains a resin that gives it a strong, hard, sticking quality. Epoxy glue is very strong. Epoxy enamel is a very durable type of paint.
Epoxy is sometimes also used as a noun to refer to epoxy glue.

escalator *noun*
An escalator is a moving staircase. It is **powered** by an **electric motor**. The stairs are made of metal and are hinged together to make an endless belt, for carrying passengers up or down.
We used the escalator in the department store to go from the first floor to the second.

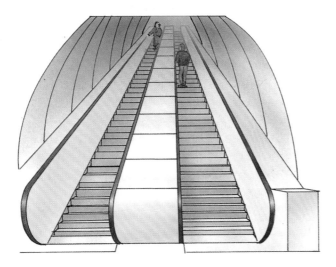

escapement clock *noun*
An escapement clock is a clock with a **spring mechanism** that is wound with a **key**. The energy which pushes the hands around is stored in the spring and allowed to escape a little at a time.
She lost the key to the escapement clock.

escape wheel *noun*
An escape wheel is a part of the **anchor escapement** of a **watch** or **clock**. It is a toothed wheel. As the anchor rocks backward and forward, it catches and turns one tooth of the wheel at a time.
The ticking sound of a clock is made by the movements of the escape wheel.

etching *noun*
Etching is a way of making designs on metal. It is done by two methods. One method is to use a sharp instrument to cut into the metal. The other is to cover part of the metal with wax and then place the metal in acid, which eats away the uncovered parts.
Etching is sometimes used to make plates from which pictures are printed.
etch *verb*

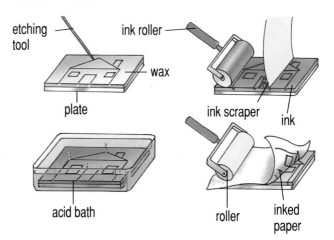

etching tool
ink roller
wax
plate
ink scraper
ink
acid bath
roller
inked paper

evaporator *noun*
An evaporator is part of a **refrigerator** or **freezer**. It is a **coil** into which a liquid called freon is **pumped** at high pressure. As the liquid enters the evaporator, its pressure drops. As the pressure drops, the liquid turns into a gas, which takes in, or absorbs, heat from inside the refrigerator. All liquids absorb heat as they evaporate. In the process, any food or liquid that has been stored in the regrigerator, loses heat. This keeps stored products fresh.
The evaporator in a freezer is sometimes called the cooling coil.

excavator   *noun*
An excavator, or steam shovel, is a **machine** for digging. It is **powered** by a **diesel engine**. An excavator is fitted with a long arm that has a metal shovel at the end. The driver can control the movements of the shovel from the cab by using **hydraulic rams**.
The excavator was digging the foundations for a new building.

exhaust ► **exhaust gas**

exhaust gas   *noun*
Exhaust gas is the mixture of waste gases that comes out of the exhaust pipe of an **engine**. A **steam engine** produces steam as its exhaust gas. The exhaust gas from **internal combustion engines** is poisonous. It includes carbon monoxide, nitrogen oxide, and lead.
There was a great deal of traffic and the air was full of exhaust gas.

exploration rig   *noun*
An exploration or drilling rig is a kind of **oil rig**. It is a structure used in the search for **oil**. An exploration rig is a tall metal tower that supports a **drill**. Exploration rigs used at sea are built on platforms. They also have living quarters for the workers and a place for **helicopters** to land.
News came from the exploration rig that oil had been discovered.

extruder   *noun*
An extruder is a part of a **machine** that forms metal, **plastics**, or artificial fibers into shapes. The extruder squirts the material out of a nozzle, after which the material hardens.
Nylon is made by mixing chemicals and pushing the mixture through an extruder.

facsimile ► **fax**

fan   *noun*
A fan is an **appliance** for keeping things or people cool. It has a number of blades fixed to a **shaft**, which is turned by a **motor**. Fans that are used in buildings are powered by **electricity**.
Most car engines have a fan to cool the water in the radiator.

fax   *noun*
Fax is short for facsimile. It is a written message sent by **telephone**. A fax **machine** copies a document placed in it and sends **electric signals** to another fax machine. This produces a copy of the document.
He sent a fax in three minutes from New York to London.
fax   *verb*

ferrous   *adjective*
Ferrous describes **iron**, or any metal containing iron. Ferrous metals are **alloys** that contain large amounts of iron. They can be picked up by a magnet because magnets attract iron.
Steel is made from iron and so it is a ferrous metal.

ferry   *noun*
A ferry is a kind of **ship** that carries passengers and **vehicles** across rivers, canals, or narrow stretches of sea. Ferries usually have large openings at each end so they can be loaded and unloaded without having to turn around.
We took the ferry from Boston to Cape Cod.

fiberglass   *noun*
Fiberglass is a strong and very lightweight material made by weaving threads of spun **glass**. It is sometimes used for curtains and for furniture covers.
Some boat hulls and car bodies are made from fiberglass, mixed with plastics.

fiber optics ▶ page 51

file   *noun*
1. A file is a **tool** made of hardened metal, that is used to shape wood or metal. It has a rough surface with a diamond-shaped pattern cut into it.
He used a file to shape the metal so that it fit exactly into the hole.
2. A file is information stored on a **computer disk** or in the computer's **memory**. Every file has a name so it can be found easily.
I am starting some new work on my computer and have opened a new file.

film   *noun*
1. A film is a thin layer of a solid or a liquid. In **machines**, a film of **oil** is spread over the working parts as a **lubricant**.
There was a film of oil on top of the water.
2. A film is a strip of material called celluloid that is coated with **chemicals** that are sensitive to light. **Cameras** and **movie cameras** use film to take **photographs**.
He loaded some new film into his camera.

filter   *noun*
1. A filter is a **device** that separates solids from liquids or **gases**. Tiny holes in the filter allow the liquid or gas to pass through. Solids are left behind in the filter.
A car's air filter removes dust from the air entering the engine.
2. A filter is a **disk** of colored **glass** or **plastic** that takes in, or absorbs, different colors from light. Photographers sometimes put filters over the **lenses** of their **cameras**.
A red filter allows only the color red to pass through it.

fire alarm   *noun*
A fire alarm is a **device** tht gives a warning if fire breaks out. It can detect smoke or heat by itself, or it can be pulled by a person.
We left the building because the fire alarm sounded.

firearm   *noun*
A firearm is a weapon that uses **bullets** as ammunition. It is a **gun** or pistol. Normally a fire arm is a pistol that can be carried by just one person. Firearms can be carried legally by adults in some countries but not in others.
They showed their firearm skill in the Olympic rifle competition.

fire extinguisher   *noun*
A fire extinguisher is a **device** for putting out a fire. It sprays water, **chemicals**, or foam on the flames, putting them out by cutting off their oxygen supply and cooling the burning material.
He sprayed foam from the fire extinguisher onto the flames.

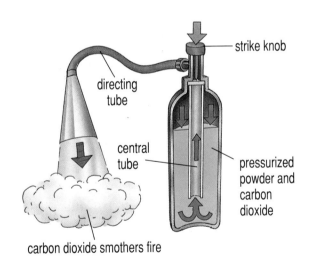

strike knob
directing tube
central tube
pressurized powder and carbon dioxide
carbon dioxide smothers fire

firefighting ▶ page 52

flight deck   *noun*
A flight deck is the part of an **aircraft** where the controls are found.
The pilot and copilot sat on the flight deck.

flight simulator ▶ page 54

fiber optics   *plural noun*

Fiber optics is a way of sending messages by light waves. The messages travel along thin fibers made of **glass**. Special equipment turns the **electric signals** that make up the messages into flickers, or pulses, of light. *Fiber optics are often used instead of copper cables for carrying telephone messages.*

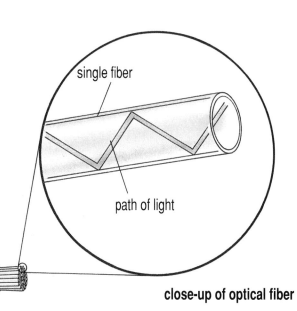

single fiber

path of light

close-up of optical fiber

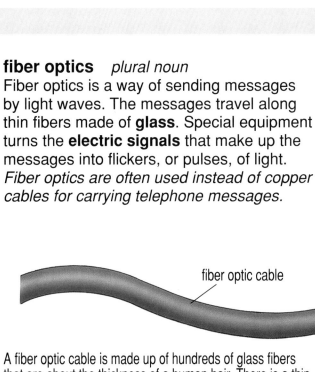

fiber optic cable

A fiber optic cable is made up of hundreds of glass fibers that are about the thickness of a human hair. There is a thin, outer covering of a different kind of glass. This makes sure that the laser light bounces from side to side without escaping.

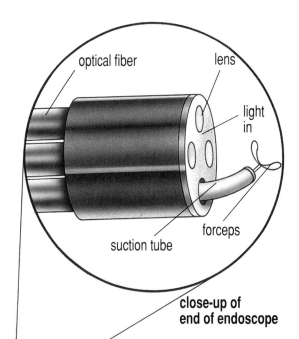

optical fiber

lens

light in

forceps

suction tube

close-up of end of endoscope

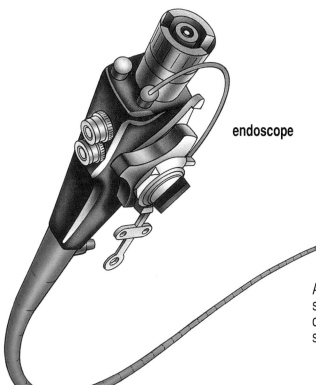

endoscope

An endoscope has a fiber optic cable that allows a doctor to see inside a patent's body. It is used in throat and stomach operations. A laser beam passing along the cable can make small cuts inside the body.

firefighting *noun*
Firefighting is the work of putting out fires.
Many different **machines** and other kinds of
equipment are used.
Firefighting is dangerous work.
Firefighting *adjective*

An elevating platform truck can lift
firefighters up to spray water onto very tall
buildings. Hydraulic rams raise the boom
with the platform on the end.

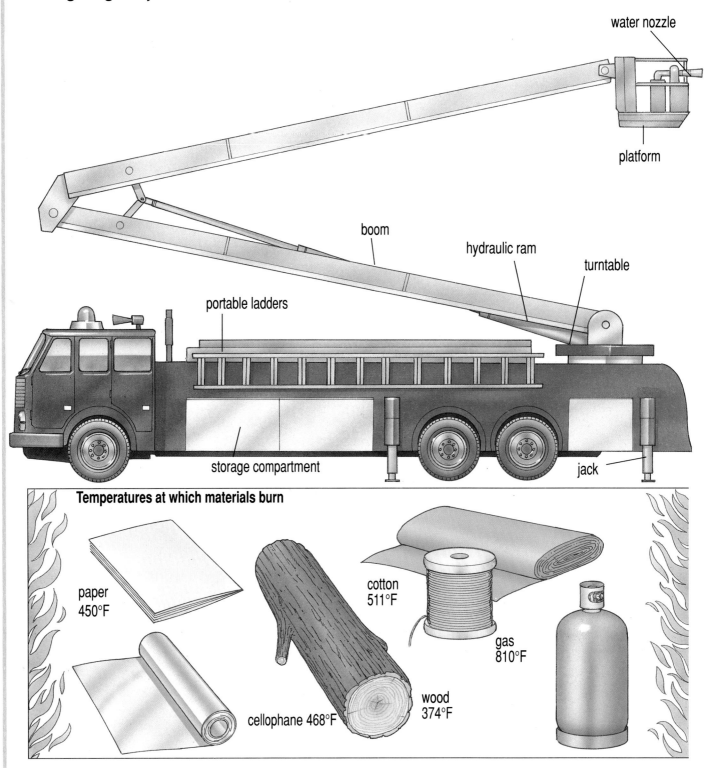

water nozzle

platform

boom

hydraulic ram

turntable

portable ladders

storage compartment

jack

Temperatures at which materials burn

paper
450°F

cellophane 468°F

wood
374°F

cotton
511°F

gas
810°F

Steam pumps were used to fight fires from the mid-1800s to the early 1900s.

Modern protective clothing allows some firefighters to walk through flames.

Some firefighting equipment

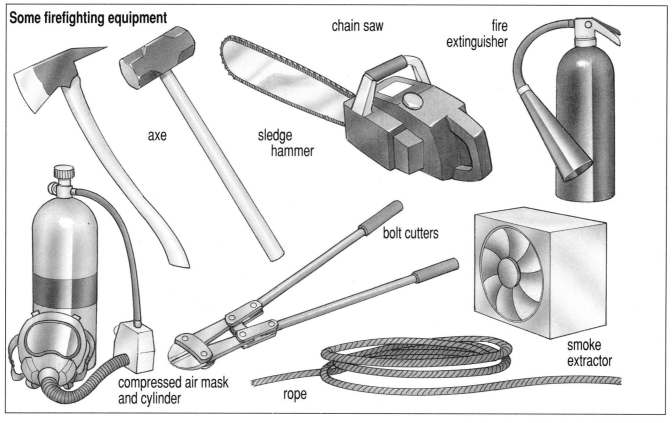

axe

sledge hammer

chain saw

fire extinguisher

bolt cutters

smoke extractor

compressed air mask and cylinder

rope

flight simulator *noun*

A flight simulator is a **machine** that copies the actions of an **aircraft** in flight. Flight simulators stay on the ground. They are used to train pilots.

She learned how to land and take off in a flight simulator.

The pilot sits in a cockpit, which has controls like those in a real airplane. A hydraulic system moves the platform to copy the movements of an airplane.

Three projectors produce a computer image on the screen that is three-dimensional. This means the image has depth, as well as height and width.

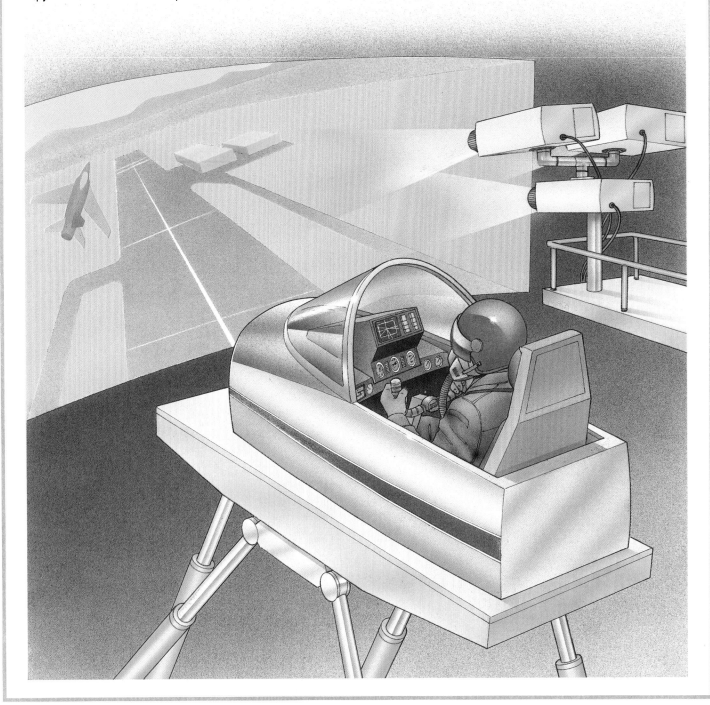

floppy disk *noun*
A floppy disk is used with a **computer**. It is a magnetic disk inside a stiff, **plastic** envelope. A floppy disk is used to store information for the computer to work with.
He put the floppy disk into the disk drive of the computer.

flow chart *noun*
A flow chart is a kind of diagram that shows the different stages at which a task must be carried out.
He used a flow chart to plan how to solve the problem.

fluorescent light *noun*
A fluorescent light is a lamp that lights when an **electric current** passes through **gas** in a sealed tube. The gas is a mixture of argon and mercury vapor. Most fluorescent lights shine a bright white.
The factory was brightly lit by fluorescent lights.

flywheel *noun*
A flywheel is a part of some **engines**. It is a heavy **wheel** that is made to spin by the running engine. A flywheel stores energy to even out the **power** produced by the **pistons**.
They saw the machine's flywheel spinning round.

focal plane shutter *noun*
A focal plane shutter is a part of some **cameras**. It controls the length of time that the **film** is exposed to the light when a **photograph** is taken.
She set the focal plane shutter to expose the film for a fraction of a second.

food processor *noun*
A food processor is an **appliance**. It chops, mixes, or minces food for use in cooking. A food processor has an **electric motor** and a large bowl.
She used her food processor to slice the fruit for the pie.

force *noun*
Force is a push or a pull. Forces make things move or change their shape. They are released by different kinds of energy.
Magnetic force made the iron filings cling to the magnet.

forklift *noun*
A forklift is a large **machine** used to lift objects up, or put them down and move them from place to place. It has a double-pronged platform at the front that can be raised and lowered by using **hydraulic rams**. The driver operates the controls from a cab, or while walking behind.
There were several forklifts moving around the factory floor.

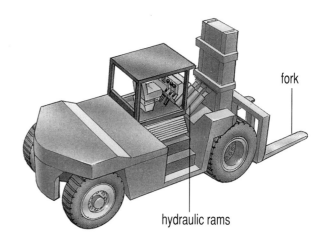

fork

hydraulic rams

fossil fuel *noun*
A fossil fuel is a solid, liquid, or **gas** fuel that was formed by plants that lived millions of years ago. Fossil fuels are used to provide energy. **Coal**, **oil**, and **natural gas** are all examples of fossil fuels.
Fossil fuels are dug or pumped from underground.

foundry *noun*
A foundry is a kind of factory where metal and **glass** objects are made. The metal or glass is heated to a very high temperature until it melts. It is then poured into molds, which give the objects their shape.
Cast-iron pots and pans are made in a foundry.

four-color printing   *noun*
Four-color printing is a method of printing full-color pictures by using four basic colors – red, blue, yellow, and black. Pictures are broken down into tiny dots, each of which is one of the four basic colors. Then, when printed on a special four-color press, the tiny dots can combine to form any color that is desired.
The book you are now reading is an example of four-color printing.

four-stroke engine   *noun*
A four-stroke engine is a kind of **internal combustion engine**. The four strokes are movements of a **piston** inside the engine. The piston sucks in a mixture of air and **fuel** and **compresses** it. Then the piston moves down as the mixture of air and fuel burns and expands.
Most cars are powered by four-stroke engines.

four-wheel drive   *noun*
Four-wheel drive is a way in which some **vehicles** are powered. **Power** from the **engine** is passed to all four **wheels**.
Four-wheel-drive vehicles can drive easily over rough or muddy ground.

fractional distillation   *noun*
Fractional distillation is a way of separating a mixture of several liquids. The mixture is boiled, and the vapor rises inside a **fractionating column**. The vapor forms into different liquids at different levels of the column, as the temperature lowers.
Many different products are made from oil by fractional distillation.

fractionating column   *noun*
A fractionating column is part of an **oil refinery**. It is a tall tower that is hot at the bottom and cooler at the top. Trays at different levels collect products separated by **fractional distillation**.
Products are pumped away from the fractionating column to be stored.

freezer   *noun*
A freezer is an electrical **appliance** found in many homes. A freezer stores food at a low temperature. The food is frozen so that it stays fresh for a long time. Sometimes part of a refrigerator, a freezer works by pumping heat away from the food inside it.
We stored the ice cream in the freezer.

friction   *noun*
Friction occurs when moving objects rub against each other. Friction makes them slow down and also produces heat. **Lubricants**, such as **oil**, are used in **machines** to reduce the friction between their moving parts.
Friction between the brake pads and discs caused the car to slow down quickly.

fridge ► **refrigerator**

frigate   *noun*
A frigate is a kind of **warship**. It is smaller than a destroyer and is used chiefly to escort other naval ships.
They toured the frigate and saw how the guns were fired.

fuel   *noun*
Fuel is a substance that is burned to provide energy. The fuel for **internal combustion engines** is **petroleum** or **diesel fuel**. **Uranium** is a fuel that is used to **generate electricity** in **nuclear power stations**.
Coal and gas are kinds of fuel.

function   *noun*
1. A function is the purpose to which a **machine** or **device** is put.
The function of a refrigerator is to keep food cool.
2. A function is a process used in **calculation**. Addition and subtraction are functions. **Electronic calculators** have **keys** that are pressed to choose different functions.
We found the total by pressing the function key for addition.

funnel *noun*
1. A funnel is another word for a smokestack. It is a pipe from which an **engine**'s **exhaust gases** are released.
Steam puffed out of the ship's funnel.
2. A funnel is an instrument that is used for pouring liquids into small openings. It is wide at the top and narrow at the bottom.
He poured gasoline into the car through a funnel.

furnace *noun*
A furnace is a **machine** for heating things. It burns **fuel** or uses **electricity** to produce great heat. Furnaces are used to heat water and melt metals.
He shoveled more coal into the furnace to raise the temperature.

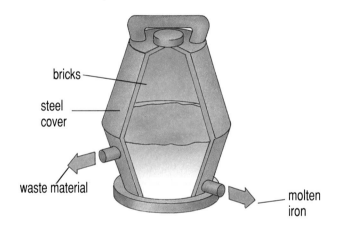

bricks
steel cover
waste material
molten iron

fuselage *noun*
A fuselage is the body of an **aircraft**. It includes the **flight deck**.
The fuselage contains the passenger compartments and the baggage hold.

galvanize *verb*
Galvanize means to protect **iron** and **steel** by giving them a coating of molten zinc. The zinc keeps air away from the iron or steel and stops it from rusting.
Nails used for roofing are galvanized so that they will not rust.

gantry *noun*
A gantry is a kind of **crane** built into the ceiling of a factory or warehouse. Chains hanging from the gantry can move objects around the factory floor.
They were careful to avoid the hook hanging from the gantry in the warehouse.

gas *noun*
A gas is a form of matter. A gas always spreads out to fill its container. It is easy to **compress** a gas. Oxygen and carbon dioxide are two different kinds of gas. Some gases are used as **fuel** for **machines**.
Butane gas is a fuel used in camping stoves.

gas laser *noun*
A gas laser is a **device** that uses a mixture of **gases**, such as neon and helium, to produce intense light energy.
Gas lasers are used in laser light shows.

gaslight *noun*
Gaslight was a form of lighting used in houses and other buildings before **electricity**. Gas was pumped through pipes and lit in special fixtures that hung from ceilings and walls.
Gaslight was more dangerous than electric lighting.

gasohol   *noun*
Gasohol is a liquid **fuel**. It is a mixture of **petroleum** and alcohol. The alcohol is made from sugar cane or grain.
Gasohol is sold as car fuel in some countries.

gasoline   *noun*
Gasoline is the **fuel** used in a **gasoline engine**. It is a **fossil fuel** which comes from **petroleum**.
Gasoline is highly flammable.

gastroscope   *noun*
A gastroscope is an instrument used by doctors in hospitals. It is a hollow tube that is passed down through a person's mouth into his or her stomach. Using mirrors, doctors can study the inside of the stomach.
The doctor used a gastroscope to find out whether the patient had a stomach ulcer.

gas turbine   *noun*
A gas turbine is a **machine** that produces energy. It burns a mixture of **fuel** and **compressed air**. This produces hot **gases** that rush through a turbine as they expand. The turbine turns a **drive shaft**, which is attached to it.
Jet aircraft are powered by gas turbine engines.

gate   *noun*
A gate is a kind of switch found in a **computer**. A gate controls the flow of **electric current** through the computer's **integrated circuit**. This control makes the computer program work properly.
A computer contains thousands of gates in a very small space.

gear ► page 60

gearbox   *noun*
A gearbox is a part of an **engine**. It contains **shafts** with a set of **gears** on each. The shafts can spin at different speeds so that the **power** can be used efficiently.
The gearbox is connected to the engine.

gearing   *noun*
Gearing is the transfer of **power** from an **engine** to the **drive shaft** of a **machine**. Low gearing is used to start a machine moving. High gearing is used for greater speed.
The racing car could reach such high speeds because it had high gearing.

gearshift   *noun*
A gearshift is a control found in an **engine**. It is used to change from one **gear** to another. This sends maximum **power** from the engine to the **drive shaft** of a **machine**.
Once the car was moving, she used the gearshift to change into second gear.

generator   *noun*
A generator is a **machine** for making **electricity**. It has a **shaft** that is turned by an **engine** or **turbine**. This movement makes **electric current** flow into wires that are connected to the generator.
There was no electricity because the generator at the power station broke down.
generate   *verb*

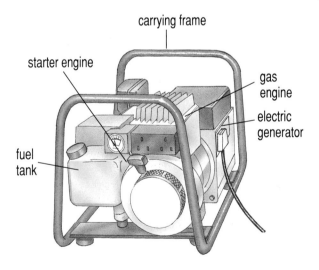

carrying frame
starter engine
gas engine
electric generator
fuel tank

glass   *noun*
Glass is a hard, solid substance made from sand and other materials. When melted, or molten, glass can be made into plates for windows, or into such objects as drinking glasses and test tubes.
Glass breaks easily because it is so brittle.

glider *noun*
A glider is a kind of **aircraft** that has no **engine**. A glider is launched either by being towed by a powered aircraft or by being shot from the ground by a kind of catapult. Once it is launched, it is kept aloft by rising air currents.
When the towrope was released, the glider soared into the sky.

glycerin *noun*
Glycerin is a thick liquid that dissolves in water. It is used as a **lubricant** in **machines** for making cloth and food.
The ice cream machine was lubricated by glycerin to avoid spoiling the ice cream with oil.

gravure printing *noun*
Gravure printing is a kind of printing process. The type or picture to be printed is **etched** into a printing plate. When ink is wiped over the surface, some stays in the etched parts and is printed onto the paper.
The color magazine was produced by gravure printing.

grinder *noun*
A grinder is a **machine tool** that is used to shape metal. **Gears** are made by grinding steel **disks** into shape using rough-surfaced materials called abrasives.
The mechanic made a new part for the machine by grinding a piece of metal.

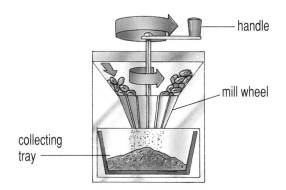

handle
mill wheel
collecting tray

guitar, electric ► **electric guitar**

gun *noun*
A gun is a **device** that fires objects from a tube. Guns can fire shot, shells, or **bullets**. Special kinds of guns are used to shoot **rivets** into sheets of metal to join them together.
The race began when he fired the starting gun.

gunmetal *noun*
Gunmetal is a strong metal made mostly from **copper** with some **tin**. Gunmetal was once used to make cannons, but now is used to make parts of **machines** that need strength but where **steel** cannot be used.
Gunmetal is a kind of bronze.

gyrocompass *noun*
A gyrocompass is a kind of compass used in **ships** and **aircraft**. It contains a **wheel** that spins freely on an **axle**, which always points in the same direction. The gyrocompass has a **dial** that is read like that of a regular **compass**.
The pilot looked at the gyrocompass.

gyroscope *noun*
A gyroscope is a **wheel** that spins. Once it is moving, it is difficult to tilt. A **gyrocompass** contains a gyroscope.
Gyroscopes are used to keep ships steady in rough seas.
gyroscopic *adjective*

gear *noun*

A gear is a **wheel** with teeth called **cogs** around its edge. Its teeth fit, or mesh, with the teeth of other gears to make them turn. Gears use the energy produced by an **engine** to turn wheels or **propellers**. They can also change the direction of a **force**. *High gear is used when a car is traveling at full speed on a clear, level road.*

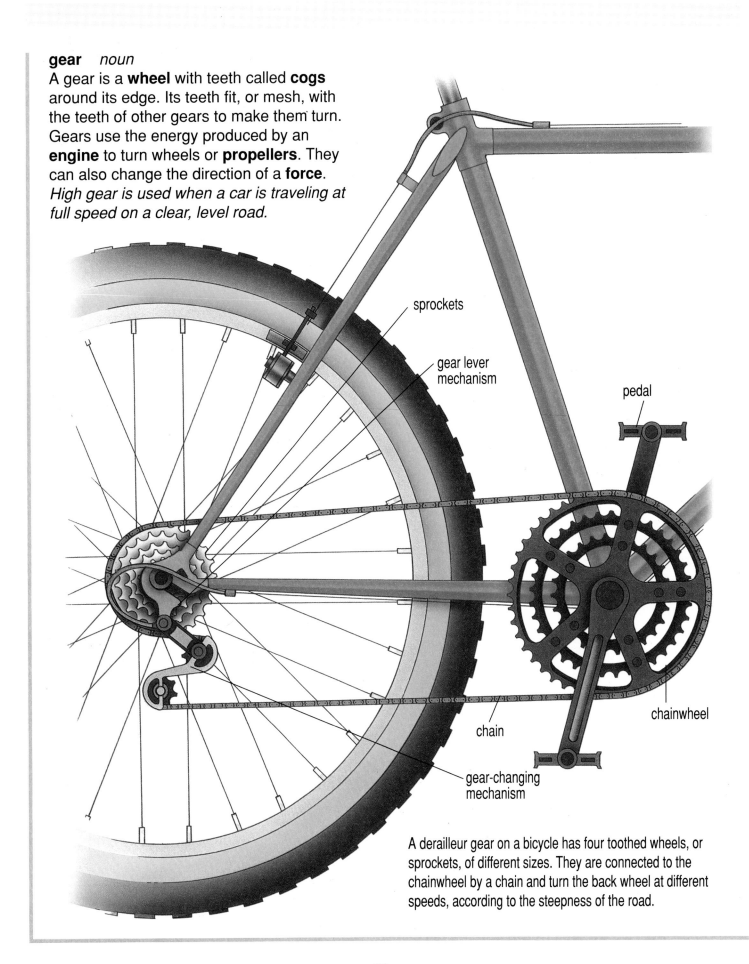

sprockets

gear lever mechanism

pedal

chainwheel

chain

gear-changing mechanism

A derailleur gear on a bicycle has four toothed wheels, or sprockets, of different sizes. They are connected to the chainwheel by a chain and turn the back wheel at different speeds, according to the steepness of the road.

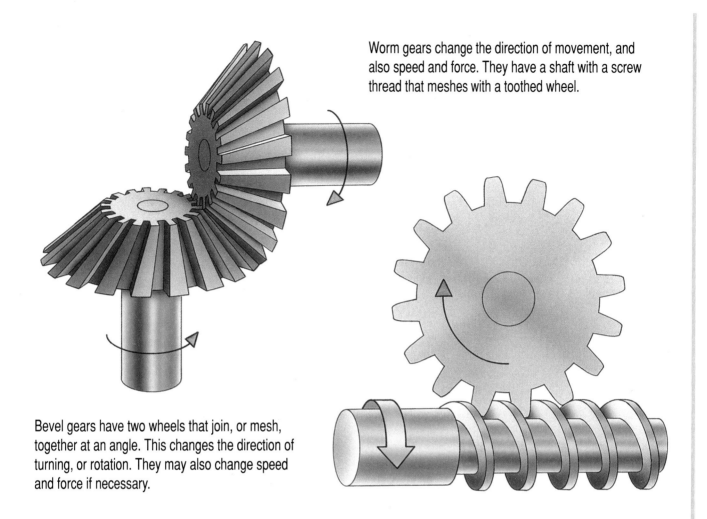

Worm gears change the direction of movement, and also speed and force. They have a shaft with a screw thread that meshes with a toothed wheel.

Bevel gears have two wheels that join, or mesh, together at an angle. This changes the direction of turning, or rotation. They may also change speed and force if necessary.

Rack and pinion gears change turning, or rotary, motion to to-and-fro, or reciprocating, motion. One wheel, called the pinion, meshes with a sliding, toothed rack.

hair dryer   *noun*

A hair dryer is an electrical **appliance**. It contains a **fan**, an **electric motor**, and a small **heater**. The fan blows warm air onto the hair of the person using the dryer.
She used a hair dryer on her hair, which had gotten wet in the rain.

hairspring   *noun*

A hairspring is part of a **watch**. It is a thin metal wire **spring** that provides the **power** to move the watch's hands.
His watch does not work because the hairspring has broken.

halogen lamp   *noun*

A halogen lamp is a kind of electric **light bulb** that gives off more light than an ordinary **bulb**. A halogen lamp contains iodine, which allows the filament inside the bulb to be brighter and hotter.
The room was lit by one halogen lamp.

hammer   *noun*

A hammer is a **tool**. It has two parts, the handle and the head. Some hammers are used to drive nails into surfaces. Others are used to beat metal into shape.
He used a hammer to drive a nail into the wall.

hand drill   *noun*

A hand drill is a **tool** used to make holes in wood. It has a **ratchet** that is turned with a handle. The ratchet turns a metal bit, or **drill**, which bores into the wood.
The carpenter took the hand drill out of the toolbox.

hang glider   *noun*

A hang glider is a kind of **aircraft**. Its wings are fixed to a light metal frame. The pilot hangs underneath in a harness. Some hang gliders are fitted with small **engines**. These are called microlights.
Hang gliders are launched into the wind down a steep slope.

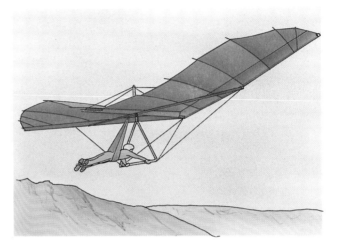

hard copy   *noun*

Hard copy is information that is printed onto paper. It is produced by a **computer** or a **fax machine**.
She used a printer to make a hard copy of the file on the floppy disk.

hard disk   *noun*

A hard disk stores information in some kinds of **computers**. This is done by using **electric signals** on a magnetic surface. Unlike a **floppy disk**, a hard disk cannot be removed from a computer. Hard disks can normally store more information than a floppy disk of the same size.
The hard disk spins at high speed inside the computer.

hardware   *noun*

Hardware is all the working parts of a **computer**. The **disk drive**, the **central processing unit**, the **input devices**, such as the **keyboard**, and the **output** devices, such as the **printer**, are all hardware.
She looked at the instruction book to find out how to connect the computer's hardware.

harvesters   *noun*
Harvesters are **machines** that gather farm crops when they are ripe. They are either pulled by **tractors** or have their own **engines**.
The harvester dug up the sugar beets and cut the tops off.

headphones   *noun*
Headphones are **appliances** used to hear sounds without disturbing other people. Headphones can be connected to a **tape recorder** or **record player** and work like a **telephone receiver**.
He listened to his new album on his headphones.

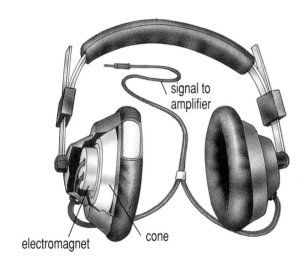

signal to amplifier

electromagnet   cone

heart-lung machine   *noun*
A heart-lung machine is a **device** used in hospitals. It copies the action of the human heart and lungs and helps to keep a person alive during a serious illness or an operation.
The hospital's operating room was equipped with a heart-lung machine.

heater   *noun*
A heater is any **device** that warms things. **Radiators**, electric fires, and **coke boilers** are all heaters. Special heaters can be put in trains and airplanes, for example, so that passengers can travel in comfort when the weather is cold.
The electric heater warmed up the room.

heat exchanger   *noun*
A heat exchanger is a **device** that moves heat from one place to another. **Air conditioners** often contain heat exchangers.
The office was kept cool by a heat exchanger.

helical gear   *noun*
A helical gear is a **gearwheel** whose teeth are set at an angle to the **shaft**. When they are moving, helical gears make less noise than gears with straight teeth.
The car's gearbox was fitted with helical gears so it would run quietly.

helicopter   *noun*
A helicopter is a kind of **aircraft**. It has **rotor blades** above the **fuselage** that support it in the air.
A helicopter can take off or land by moving straight up or down.

hi-fi   *noun*
Hi-fi is short for high fidelity. High fidelity recordings of music sound almost like the original performance.
She bought some new hi-fi equipment.

hinge   *noun*
A hinge is a **device** that allows a door to open and close. It is usually made of metal. The two parts of the hinge are joined by a rod, or hinge pin, and move freely around it. Hinges can be found on doors, gates, covers, and lids.
The door swung on its hinges.

hoist *noun*
A hoist is a **machine** for lifting large objects, such as cargo. Hoists are used on **ships** to move goods in and out of the hull. They are **powered** by an **electric motor**.
The sailor raised the crates on a hoist to load them into the waiting truck.

horn *noun*
A horn is a **device** that makes a loud noise. Horns are used to give a warning. They are fitted to road **vehicles**, **ships**, and sometimes to **machines** in factories. They may be **powered** by **electricity** or **compressed air**.
The ship sounded its horn in case it could not be seen in the thick fog.

horsepower *noun*
Horsepower is a measure of the speed at which work is done. One horsepower is equal to raising a load of 33,000 pounds one foot in one minute. The abbreviation for horsepower is hp.
The car was equipped with a 100-horsepower engine.

hot-air balloon *noun*
A hot-air balloon is a kind of **aircraft**. It has a **nylon** balloon open at the bottom, and a **burner** that fills it with hot air. The balloon rises because the hot air inside it is lighter than the cooler air outside. A basket is slung underneath the balloon to carry passengers and the burner.
He turned on the burner and the hot-air balloon began to rise.

hovercraft *noun*
A hovercraft is a **vehicle** that can be used over water, marshy ground, or flat land. It is **powered** by a **gas turbine** or **gasoline engine**. Fans beneath it make a cushion of air on which the hovercraft floats. **Propellers** on deck push the hovercraft forward.
A flexible curtain, called a skirt, keeps the cushion of air under a hovercraft as it travels along.

hub *noun*
A hub is the center of a **wheel**. It **rotates** around the **axle**.
The spokes of a bicycle wheel connect the hub to the rim.

hydraulic *adjective*
Hydraulic describes **machines** that are operated by the movement of liquids. Liquid under pressure is made to move a **piston** inside a **cylinder**. Because liquid cannot be **compressed**, great **force** can be released with little effort.
Most automobiles have hydraulic brakes.
hydraulics *noun*

hydraulic engine *noun*
A hydraulic engine is a **machine** that produces movement by means of pressure from a fluid. It is used to drive machinery, such as jacks and hoists, or move heavy loads.
The power steering of an automobile is driven by a hydraulic engine.

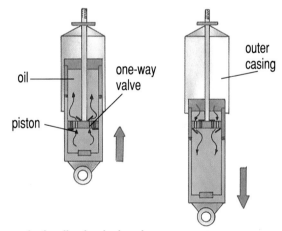

oil
one-way valve
piston
outer casing

hydraulic shock absorber

hydraulic fluid *noun*
Hydraulic fluid is used in hydraulic **machines**, such as a **forklift**. It is usually a type of **oil**. Modern hydraulic **engines** use fluids that do not freeze at low temperatures. These fluids include oil, certain silicones, and some **gases**.
He filled up the container of hydraulic fluid to make sure that the brakes worked properly.

hydraulic gearboxes   *plural noun*
Hydraulic gearboxes are parts of some cars that use **hydraulic fluid** to send **power** from the **engine** to the **drive shaft**.
A car with hydraulic gears does not need a clutch.

hydraulic jack   *noun*
A hydraulic jack is a **device** that uses the pressure of a liquid forced through an opening to lift an object. It has a platform that is placed under the object to be lifted. A **lever** works a **piston**, which makes the platform rise.
The mechanic used a hydraulic jack to change the car's tire.

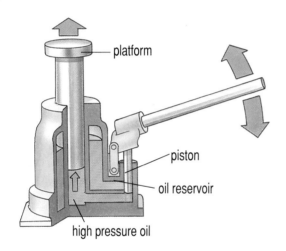
platform
piston
oil reservoir
high pressure oil

hydraulic press   *noun*
A hydraulic press is a **machine** that shapes sheets of metal. It uses **hydraulic power** to press the sheets down with great **force** onto a shaped surface. A hydraulic jack and hydraulic **brakes** use the same system as a hydraulic press.
Car bodies are shaped with a hydraulic press.

hydraulic ram   *noun*
A hydraulic ram is a **machine** used in construction work. It uses **hydraulic power** to operate a heavy weight, which rams earth into a solid mass.
The road builders used a hydraulic ram to make a firm foundation for the new road.

hydraulic robot   *noun*
A hydraulic robot is a **machine** that is used to perform tasks in factories. **Hydraulics** provide the power to operate tools automatically. They are controlled by **computers**.
Hydraulic robots fitted parts to the car bodies on the factory assembly line.

hydraulic system   *noun*
A hydraulic system is a way of transmitting **hydraulic power** over a long distance. It is made up of a number of hydraulic **cylinders** joined by pipes. A large **pump** sends **hydraulic fluid** flowing through the system.
The factory's hydraulic system provided hydraulic power for every department.

hydroelectric power   *noun*
Hydroelectric power is **electricity** that is **generated** by the power of flowing water. The water spins a **turbine**, which drives an electric **generator**.
Hydroelectric power stations need a good supply of fast-flowing water.

hydroelectric turbine   *noun*
A hydroelectric turbine is part of a **hydroelectric power** station. It has blades like fan blades, which are turned by the flow of water. The turbine's **drive shaft** powers an **electric generator**.
Water flowed from sluices in the dam into the hydroelectric turbine.

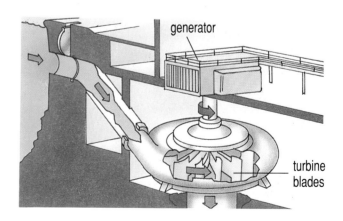
generator
turbine blades

hydrofoil ► page 66

65

hydrofoil *noun*

1. A hydrofoil is a **device** shaped like an **aircraft** wing. It is used on or under water. Because of its shape, water flows more quickly over the top surface than the bottom. *Some ocean liners are fitted with hydrofoils to keep them steady in rough seas.*

2. A hydrofoil is also a kind of **ship** that travels just above the surface of the water on hydrofoils.
A hydrofoil can reach high speeds because it is not slowed down by water resistance.

A hydrofoil is like a wing that goes through water. This hydrofoil is used by the United States Navy and carries guided missiles.

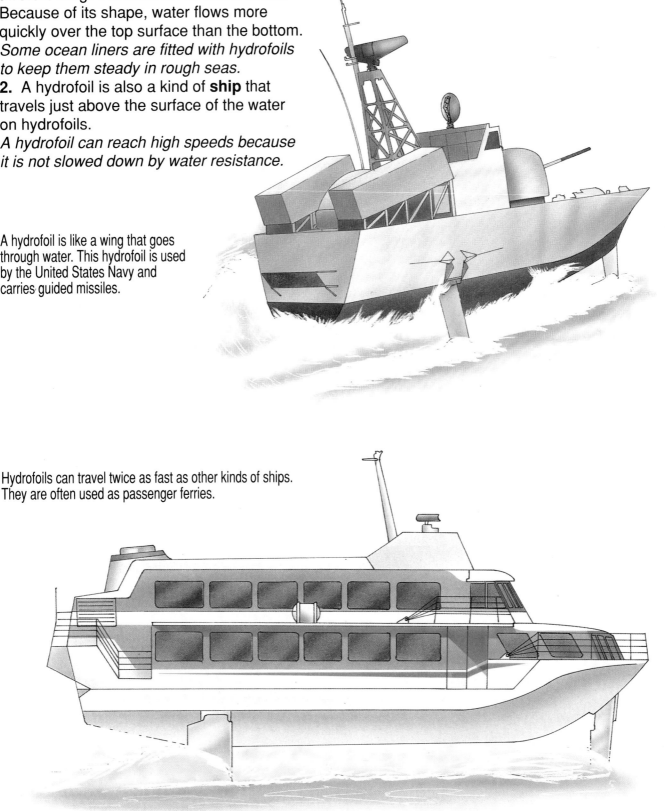

Hydrofoils can travel twice as fast as other kinds of ships. They are often used as passenger ferries.

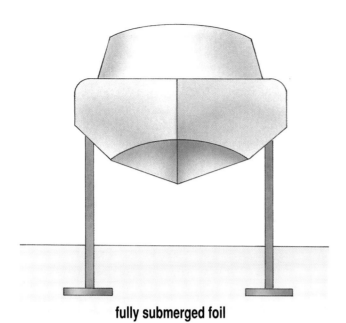

fully submerged foil

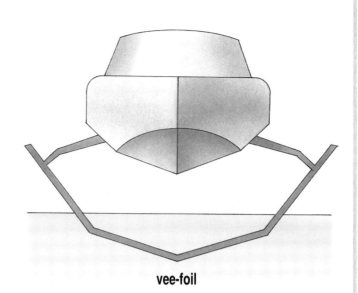

vee-foil

In fully submerged hydrofoils, the foils stay completely under water. These hydrofoils can be used in rough seas, but need stabilizers to keep them steady.

Part of the vee-foil appears above the surface of the water as the vessel moves forward. This type of hydrofoil was easier to develop than submerged ones, but can only be used in calm, coastal waters.

shallow-draft foil

ladder foil

The shallow-draft foil is fully submerged, but can keep steady without stabilizers.

The ladder foil was used in an early hydrofoil built in 1918. It set a world waterspeed record of almost 70 miles per hour. The record remained unbroken until 1963.

hydrogen bomb *noun*
A hydrogen bomb is a **nuclear weapon**. It explodes with great **force** when hydrogen atoms are joined together in the process of nuclear fusion. Hydrogen bombs have never been used in wartime.
The explosion of a hydrogen bomb produces great heat and releases enormous energy and radioactivity.

hydrophone *noun*
A hydrophone is a **device** for hearing sounds under water. It receives sound waves and converts them into **electric signals**. These signals can be seen on a **meter** or played through a **loudspeaker**.
Fishermen use hydrophones to help them find schools of fish.

hydroplane *noun*
A hydroplane is part of a **submarine**. Hydroplanes are fitted in pairs at the front and back of the hull. They look like short fins, and they can be tilted to raise or lower the submarine in the water.
Hydroplanes help a submarine to dive and surface.

hydroplane *verb*
Hydroplane is to slide along on a film of water. An ice skater hydroplanes on the film of water on top of the ice.
The accident was caused when the car hydroplaned on a patch of water in the road.

hypodermic syringe *noun*
A hypodermic syringe is a **device** that injects substances under the skin of a person or animal. It is fitted with a hollow, pointed needle. Doctors sometimes use a hypodermic syringe to inject a patient with medicine.
My doctor used a hypodermic syringe to give me a vaccine to protect me from influenza.

ignition system ► page 69

incandescent lamp *noun*
An incandescent lamp is a **light bulb** that contains a thin wire, or filament. The **electricity** that passes through the wire makes it glow.
Thomas Alva Edison was the inventor of the incandescent lamp.

inclined plane *noun*
An inclined plane is a **simple machine**. It is a sloping surface. It is easier to push an object up an inclined plane than to lift it.
A screw has an inclined plane running round it from top to bottom.

induction motor ► **linear induction motor**

inertia *noun*
Inertia is the tendency of an object to stay at rest unless a **force** acts on it to set it in motion.
The student learned that a cannonball has a greater inertia than a tennis ball because it is heavier.

information technology ► page 70

inkjet printer ► **bubblejet printer**

input *noun*
Input is information that is loaded into a **computer** through the use of **devices**, such as **keyboards**, **joysticks**, and **floppy disks**.
He used a keyboard to type input into the computer.

ignition system *noun*

An ignition system is part of some **internal combustion engines**. It uses **electricity** to make a spark, which causes the mixture of **fuel** and air in the **cylinders** to explode.
The ignition system sends bursts of electricity to the spark plugs.

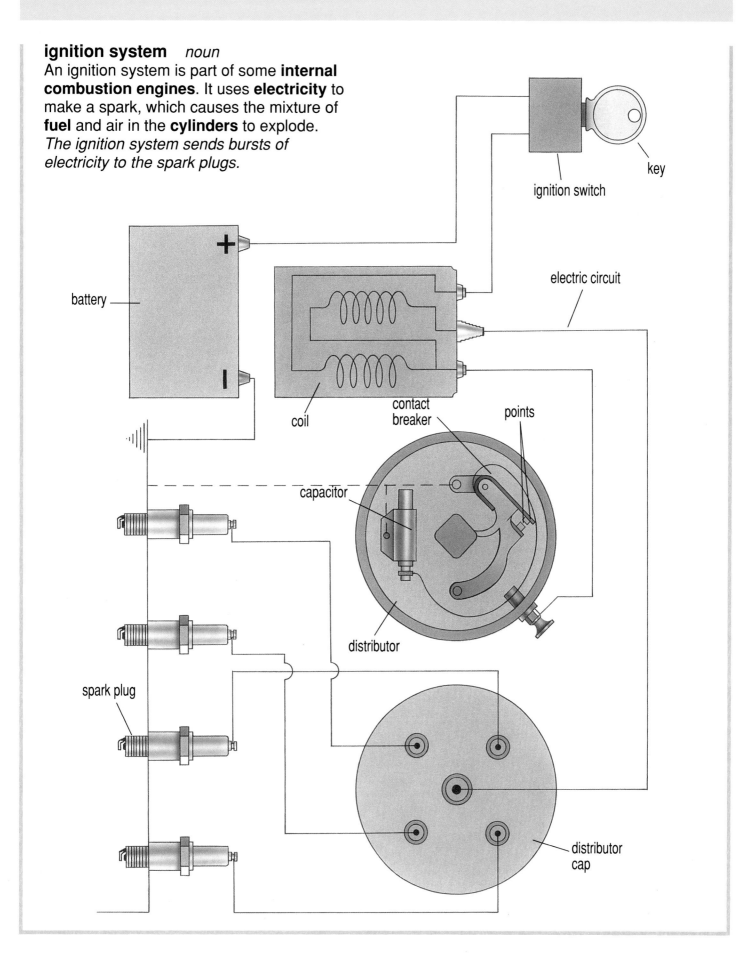

key

ignition switch

battery

electric circuit

coil

contact breaker

points

capacitor

distributor

spark plug

distributor cap

information technology *noun*
Information technology is the science that develops new forms of communication. **Computers**, **fax**, **television,** and **radio** are all products of information technology. *Information technology uses data in the form of electric signals.*

A fax machine sends and receives printed messages over telephone wires.

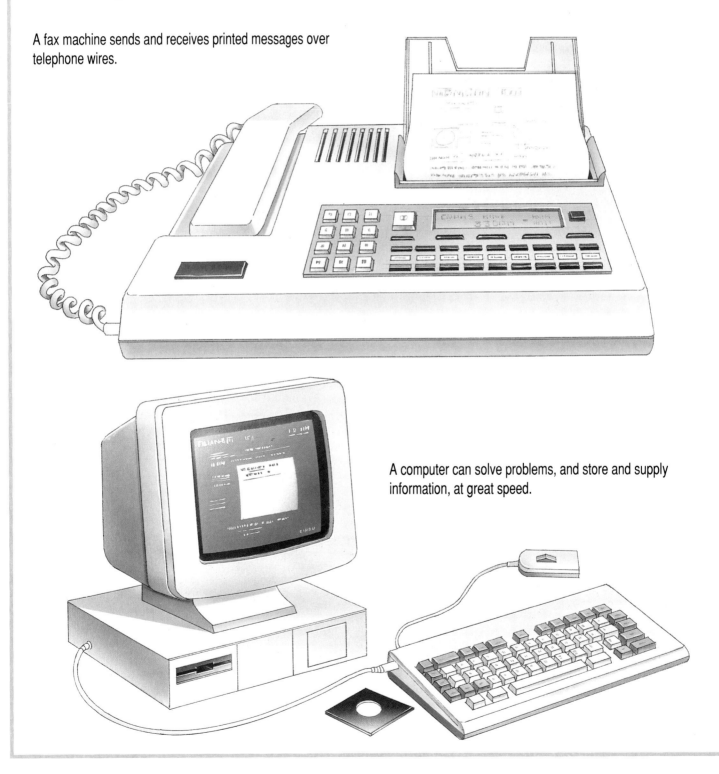

A computer can solve problems, and store and supply information, at great speed.

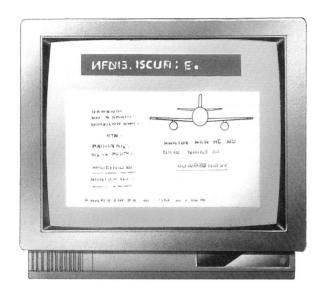

Some types of information systems allow users, such as travel agents, to key in data as well as receive it. Their terminals are connected by telephone lines to a central computer.

A radio can be tuned to different wavelengths to receive many different programs. It receives radio signals from a transmitter and changes them into sound.

A television may receive its programs in three different ways. Signals may come from a land-based transmitter through the atmosphere. They may also travel along fiber optic cables underground, or via a satellite circling Earth.

internal combustion engine *noun*

An internal combustion engine is an **engine** that burns **fuel** inside. **Gasoline** and **diesel engines**, and **gas turbines**, are internal combustion engines.

You cannot see the working parts of internal combustion engines because they are located inside.

A diesel internal combustion engine runs on diesel fuel. It does not have spark plugs to ignite the fuel as a gasoline engine does. Instead, the very high pressure inside the cylinder raises the temperature of the mixture of air and fuel until it explodes.

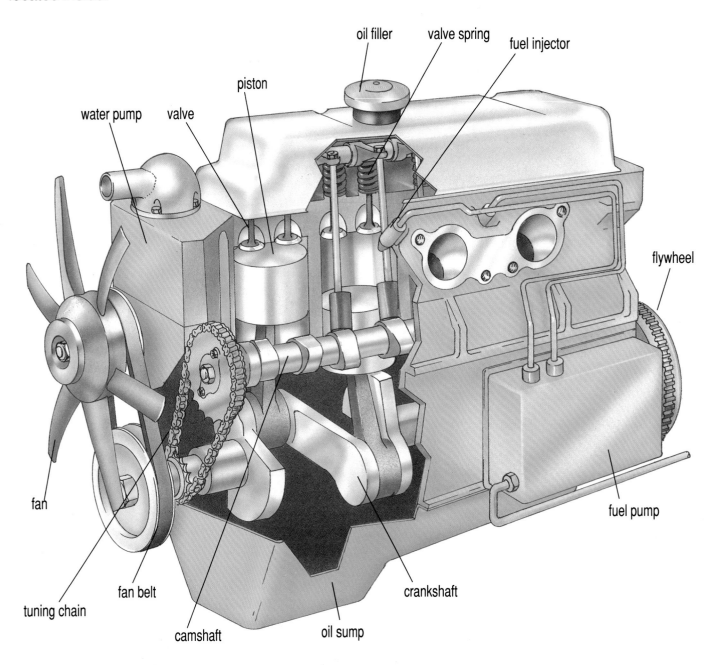

oil filler

valve spring

fuel injector

piston

water pump

valve

flywheel

fan

fan belt

tuning chain

camshaft

oil sump

crankshaft

fuel pump

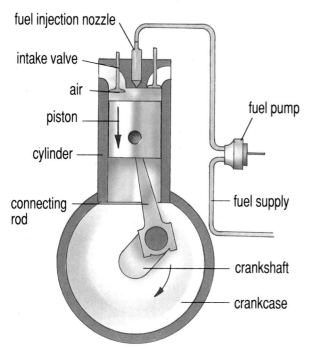

1. Intake stroke
The piston moves down and draws air into the cylinder.

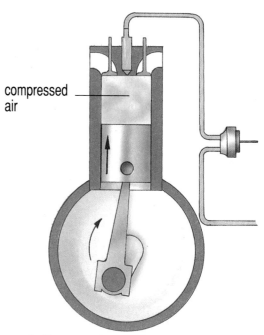

2. Compression stroke
The piston moves up and squeezes, or compresses, the air. Air temperature rises to about 900°F.

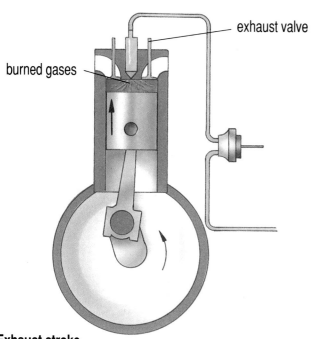

4. Exhaust stroke
Piston moves up and forces exhaust gases out of the cylinder.

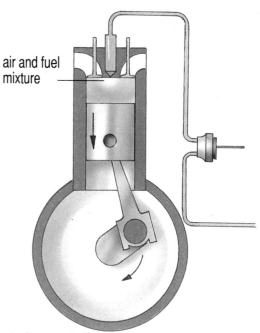

3. Power stroke
Fuel injected into cylinder where it mixes with hot air and explodes. Gases produced by explosion push piston down.

insulator *noun*

An insulator is a substance or a **device** that stops the flow of heat or **electricity**. The **plastic** covering on **electric cables** is an insulator. **Asbestos** is an insulator against heat.

The insulators on the poles prevented electricity from reaching the ground.

insulate *verb*

integrated circuit *noun*

An integrated circuit is a part of **electronic** equipment. It is a silicon chip that has **electric circuits** engraved on it. An integrated circuit is also called a chip or a microchip.

When a computer is working, thousands of signals flow through its integrated circuits.

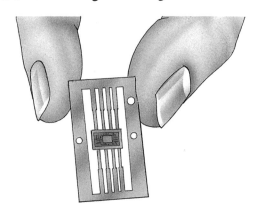

interface *noun*

An interface is part of a **computer**. It is an **electric cable** with a plug at each end, and it connects parts of the computer together.

They could not connect the monitor to the CPU because they did not have the right interface.

internal combustion engine ► page 72

inventor *noun*

An inventor is someone who uses his or her imagination to create a new **machine** or other **device**. Inventors may try to market their own inventions or they may sell them to a large company.

Alexander Graham Bell was the inventor of the telephone, in 1875.

ionizer ► **air ionizer**

iron *noun*

1. Iron is a dark gray, **ferrous** metal. **Cast iron** is brittle and breaks easily. Iron is the main ingredient in **steel**, which is used in many **machines**. Magnets attract iron.

When iron is left outside, it reacts with water vapor from the air that makes it rust.

2. An iron is an **appliance** for pressing such items as clothes and sheets. **Electricity** heats a smooth plate, which is passed over the fabric. Some irons hold water and release steam as they move.

Her dress was creased, so she pressed it with an iron.

iron lung *noun*

An iron lung is a metal **machine** used in hospitals to help sick patients breathe. An iron lung does the work of the chest muscles that the patient cannot use.

The iron lung forced air in and out of the patient's lungs.

IT ► **information technology**

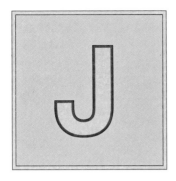

jack   *noun*

A jack is a **machine** for lifting objects from below. A car jack lifts a **wheel** off the ground so that the tire can be changed. Small jacks can be made to work by turning a handle. Larger jacks use **hydraulic power**.
She had a flat tire, so she took out the jack to change the wheel.

jet airplane   *noun*

A jet airplane is an **aircraft** fitted with **jet engines**. Most fighter aircraft and large **airliners** are jet airplanes.
The jet airplane made a loud noise as it swooped overhead.

jet engine   *noun*

A jet engine is an **engine** that sucks in air and pushes out a jet of hot **gases**. The gases come out with such **force** that they push the engine forward. The gases are produced by a **gas turbine**.
They could see the heat haze caused by the jet engines as the aircraft took off.

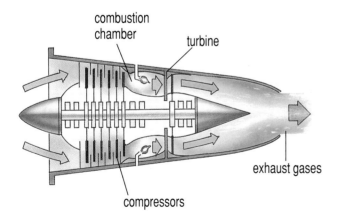

combustion chamber turbine

exhaust gases

compressors

jet pack   *noun*

A jet pack is a **device** that allows an astronaut to move about in space. It is strapped to the astronaut's back. The astronaut can make it send out a jet of **compressed air**, which pushes him in any direction he wants.
The astronaut used his jet pack to move about outside the spacecraft.

joystick   *noun*

1. A joystick, or control column, is the name for one of the controls of an **aircraft**. The pilot pushes it forward to dive, backward to climb, and left or right to turn.
After takeoff, the pilot pulled on the joystick to climb to his planned altitude.
2. A joystick is one of the **input devices** that can be used with a **computer**. It is a handle that is connected by **cable** to the computer, and it is used to control the picture on the **visual display unit**.
Joysticks are often used to play computer games.

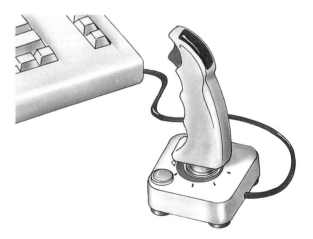

jump jet   *noun*

A jump jet is a kind of **aircraft** that can take off or land vertically. The jet thrust from its **jet engine** can be made to point downward. Some jump jets can also fly sideways or backward. Jump jets are sometimes called **vertical-takeoff-and-landing aircraft**, or VTOLs.
A jump jet does not need a runway to land on.

kerosene *noun*
Kerosene is a liquid **fuel** made from **oil**. It is used in **jet engines**. It is also used as a fuel in **heaters** and in lamps.
The jet airplane's fuel tanks were filled with kerosene.

key *noun*
1. A key is a button that is found on a **keyboard** or **keypad**. When it is pressed, it sends instructions or **data** to a **computer** or **electronic calculator**.
She pressed the addition key on her calculator to find the total.
2. A key is a small rod or strip of metal used to open a **lock**. It is cut into a shape that fits inside of the lock.
He opened the lock with his key.
key *verb*

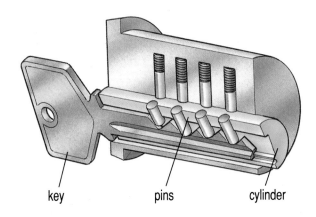

key   pins   cylinder

keyboard *noun*
A keyboard is the part of a **computer** that has rows of **keys**. Some keys have letters or numbers on them. Others carry out certain **functions**. A keyboard is a computer **input**.
A keyboard can feed data into a computer.

keypad *noun*
A keypad is a small **keyboard** with no more than 20 **keys**. An **electronic calculator** has a keypad, which is used to feed in numbers and **functions**.
The plus sign on a keypad marks the key that is used for addition.

kilobyte *noun*
A kilobyte is a unit of measurement. It is used to describe the size of the **memory** in a **computer** or the amount of **data** that can be stored on a **floppy disk** or a **hard disk**. A kilobyte is the same as 1,000 **bytes**. It is sometimes abbreviated to KB or K.
The floppy disk could hold up to 720 kilobytes of information.

kinetic energy *noun*
Kinetic energy is energy that objects have when they are moving. If an object is heavy and moves quickly, it has a large amount of kinetic energy. **Machines** that use **fuel** turn **chemical** energy into kinetic energy. Wind and flowing water also have kinetic energy.
Everything that is moving has kinetic energy.

kite *noun*
A kite is a small **device** that flies. It has **airfoils** that are supported by the flow of air over them. Kites often have a tail attached to balance them, and are controlled from the ground by a person holding a string.
We went to the beach on a windy day and flew our kites.

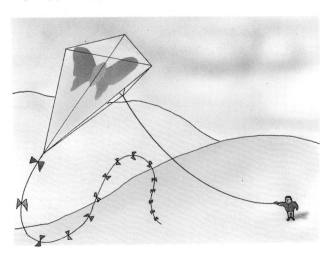

laminate   *noun*
A laminate is a material made from a number of layers that are stuck together. Laminates made from wood and **plastics** are often used for office and kitchen furniture.
The kitchen counter was made from a laminate of chipboard and plastic.
laminate   *verb*

landing gear   *noun*
The landing gear, or undercarriage, is the equipment that an **aircraft** uses when it takes off or lands. It is usually a set of **wheels** underneath the **fuselage** or wings. Most aircraft pull in, or retract, their landing gear into the fuselage when in flight.
The pilot lowered the airplane's landing gear as he approached the airport.

laser   *noun*
A laser is a **device** that produces a narrow beam of very bright, powerful light. It uses light energy to perform tasks. A laser beam can be used to cut metal. Lasers are also used by doctors to perform operations, and in **fiber optics**.
Laser light can be directed where it is needed by the use of mirrors.

laser printer   *noun*
A laser printer is an **output device** for some **computers**. **Electronic signals** from the **central processing unit** are changed into pulses of laser light. This makes images on a drum. Ink powder sticks to the images and is transferred onto paper.
She used a laser printer to copy her drawing.

laser scalpel   *noun*
A laser scalpel is an instrument used in hospitals to destroy diseased body tissue. Laser scalpels prevent the loss of blood during operations, as they do not cut blood vessels.
The surgeon used a laser scalpel to perform an operation on the boy's eye.

lathe   *noun*
A lathe is a **machine tool** used to cut, shape, or polish wood or metal. An object is held tightly in the lathe and turned around, or rotated, while special turning tools are used to work on the object. Small lathes can be **powered** by a foot pedal called a **treadle**. Larger lathes have an **electric motor**. Many parts of car **engines** are made with a lathe.
The carpenter shaped the chair leg on a lathe.

launch vehicle   *noun*
A launch vehicle is a kind of **rocket** used to send objects into space. It burns **chemicals** to provide the **power** for the first stage of the object's journey.
Clouds of burning gas poured out of the launch vehicle as the spacecraft lifted off.

lawn mower   *noun*
A lawn mower is an **appliance** for cutting grass. Some mowers have rows of blades formed into a hollow **cylinder** across the front of the **machine**. Others have disk blades fitted beneath the machine.
Some rotary lawn mowers have long, flat blades that spin flat when they cut the grass.

lawn sprinkler   *noun*
A lawn sprinkler is a **device** for sprinkling water evenly over a lawn. It is connected to a water supply. The **force** of the water pushes around a nozzle inside the sprinkler. This makes sure that each part of the lawn around the sprinkler is watered.
There had been no rain for days, so they decided to water the grass with a lawn sprinkler.

leaf spring   *noun*
A leaf spring is part of a **vehicle**. It is made up of strips of special **steel**. The ends of the spring are attached to the **chassis** of the vehicle, and it is fixed to an **axle** at the center. The leaf spring absorbs shocks from the surface on which the vehicle is traveling.
The cart was fitted with leaf springs, which made our ride more comfortable.

lens ▶ **concave lens, convex lens**

letterpress printing   *noun*
Letterpress printing is a printing process. The surface of the characters or images to be printed is raised. A film of ink is spread over the surface and then pressed onto paper.
Letterpress printing was used to produce the poster for the meeting.

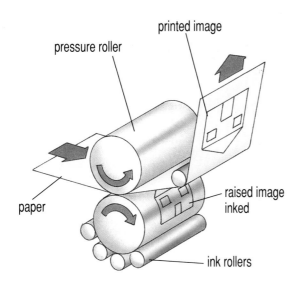

printed image
pressure roller
paper
raised image inked
ink rollers

lever ▶ page 80

light bulb   *noun*
A light bulb is a **device** which uses **electricity** to produce light. It is made of **glass**, inside of which is a thin wire called a filament, usually made of tungsten. The bulb is filled with a **gas** that stops the filament from becoming brittle.
When electricity flows through a light bulb filament, it glows brightly.

lighthouse   *noun*
A lighthouse is a tower with a bright light in it that is used to direct navigation. Some lighthouses are used to warn **ships** away from rocks. Other lighthouses are used to guide ships safely into ports.
Lighthouses often have foghorns or other signals for use during bad weather.

light meter   *noun*
A light meter is a **device** that measures amounts of light. It is used by a photographer to set a **camera** so that the **film** is properly exposed.
She used a light meter to check the camera setting needed to take the picture.

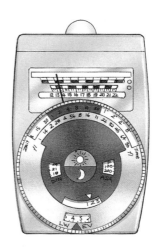

lightning rod   *noun*
A lightning rod is a length of thick wire. One end is attached to the top of a building and the other is buried in the ground.
A lightning rod carries lightning safely into the ground and prevents a building from being damaged if it is struck.

light pen   *noun*
A light pen is a **device** used in some stores and libraries. When it is passed over a **bar code**, it changes light signals from the bar code into **electric signals**. These are sent along an **electric cable** to a **computer**.
The store clerk ran her light pen over the bar code on the can to get the price, so she could charge the customer.

linear induction motor *noun*

A linear induction motor is an **electric motor** that works by making an electromagnetic field. Movable parts of a **machine** are either pushed away or pulled forward by the motor. As the pushing and pulling effects work in turn, the movable parts can travel along a track.
Sliding doors are often operated by linear induction motors.

liquid crystal display *noun*

A liquid crystal display is a **device** that lights up to show letters, numbers, or images. It looks like a very small **screen**. The display changes when different **electric signals** are fed into it. The abbreviation for liquid crystal display is LCD. LCDs are found in **electronic calculators** and in some **digital clocks** and **watches**.
The liquid crystal display on my watch showed that it was time to start leaving for school.

lithographic printing *noun*

In lithographic printing, the letters or images to be printed are marked on a printing plate with a greasy substance. The rest of the plate is made wet. When ink is rolled onto the plate, it sticks only to the greasy parts. The ink is then transferred to paper. **Offset lithography** is a special kind of lithographic printing.
Many books are produced by lithographic printing.

load *noun*

A load is a weight or **force** that is supported by a **structure** or any part of a structure. It is also a weight that another force pushes or pulls. Beams, bridges, and pillars support loads. **Levers**, **pulleys**, and other **machines** move loads. Forces produced by machines act in the opposite direction to move the load.
The bulldozer moved the load of earth from the middle to the edge of the road, so that traffic could pass.

lock *noun*

A lock is a **device** that keeps objects secure. Some locks will open only when a **key** of the right shape is inserted. Others are **combination locks** and can be opened only with a **code** number.
She turned the key in the lock.
lock *verb*

long-wave radio *noun*

Long-wave radio is a method of **transmitting** and **receiving** signals by **radio** over long distances.
We listened to a program from abroad by long-wave radio.

loom *noun*

A loom is a **weaving machine** for making cloth. It weaves threads or yarn above and below each other so that they stay tightly together. Looms are either hand-driven or power-driven. **Power** looms are usually found in factories and are run by **electricity**; they used to be run by water or steam.
They saw the looms at work making carpets.

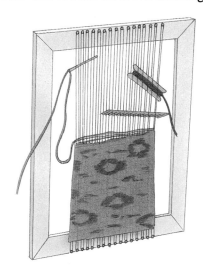

loudspeaker *noun*

A loudspeaker is a part of a **radio**, **television**, or **record player** that changes **electric signals** into sounds. The sounds come out of the front of the loudspeaker.
He turned up the volume of the loudspeaker so that he could hear the news.

lever *noun*

1. A lever is a **simple machine**. It is a bar that rests at one point called the fulcrum. Effort is applied at one end of the lever. This effort lifts a weight, or **load**, at the other end. *Seesaws and wheelbarrows are examples of a lever.*

2. A lever is a **device** used to operate **machines**. It is a kind of switch. Moving the lever makes the machine operate in a certain way. *The car's driver used the gear lever to change gears.*

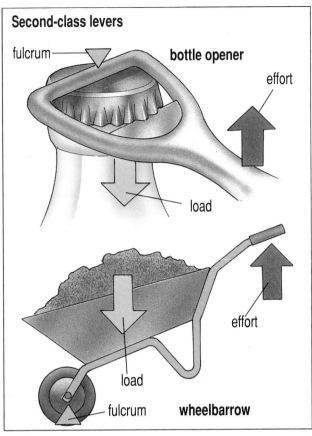

Second-class levers

fulcrum

bottle opener

effort

load

effort

effort

load

fulcrum **wheelbarrow**

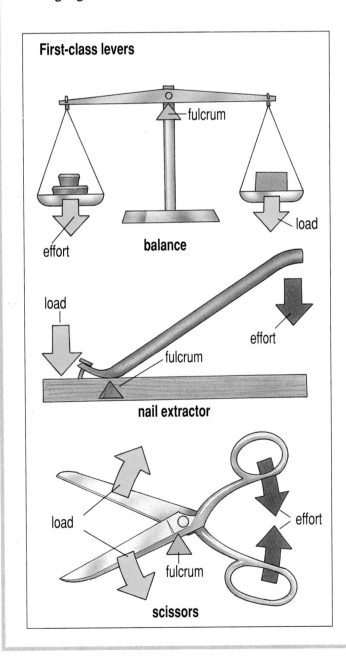

First-class levers

fulcrum

load

effort **balance**

load

effort

fulcrum

nail extractor

load

effort

fulcrum

scissors

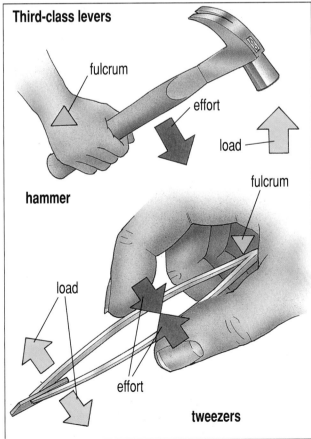

Third-class levers

fulcrum

effort

load

hammer

fulcrum

load

effort

tweezers

Multiple levers

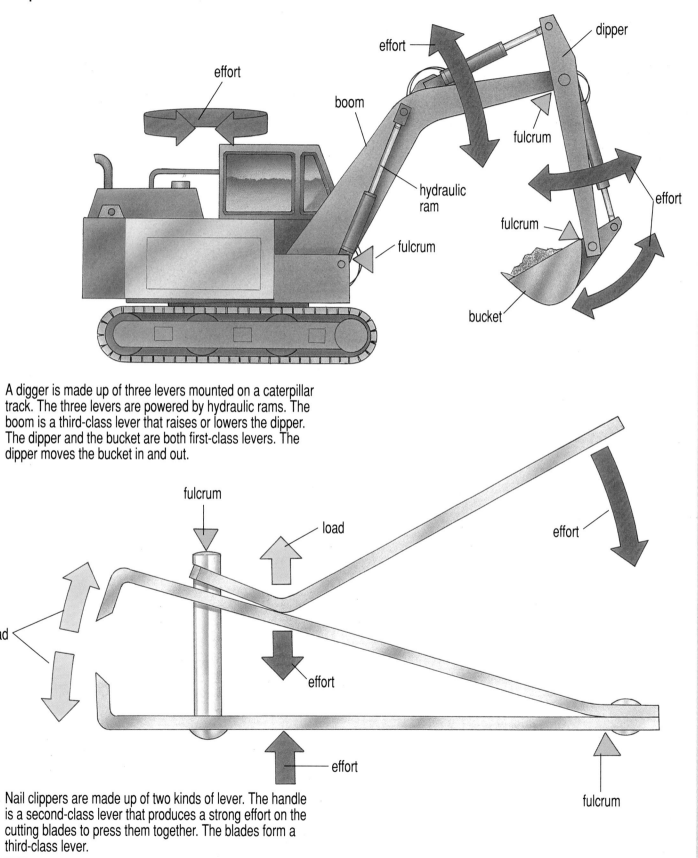

A digger is made up of three levers mounted on a caterpillar track. The three levers are powered by hydraulic rams. The boom is a third-class lever that raises or lowers the dipper. The dipper and the bucket are both first-class levers. The dipper moves the bucket in and out.

Nail clippers are made up of two kinds of lever. The handle is a second-class lever that produces a strong effort on the cutting blades to press them together. The blades form a third-class lever.

lubricant   *noun*
A lubricant is a slippery liquid. Lubricants make the moving parts of **machines** slide smoothly against each other and reduce the amount of **friction**. **Oil** is used as a lubricant in car **engines** and many other machines.
The car was not running smoothly because there was not enough lubricant in the engine.
lubricate   *verb*

machine   *noun*
A machine is any **device** that does work. It changes the direction or strength of a **force** applied to it. **Screws**, **levers**, **wheels**, wedges, **inclined planes**, and **pulleys** are all **simple machines**. These simple machines go together to make up more complicated machines, such as **engines** and **motors**. A machine is also any device that has moving parts.
A sewing machine is useful for making clothes.
machinery   *noun*

machine language   *noun*
Machine language is a set of instructions that a **computer** can use without having to translate it.
Machine language is formed in binary code.

machine tool   *noun*
A machine tool is a tool that is **powered** by a **machine**. **Lathes** and **electric drills** are examples of machine tools.
In the factory, machine tools were used to cut and shape the parts of the engine.

maglev train   *noun*
A maglev train is a **train** that runs on a special **track**. Magnetic **forces** hold the train a few millimeters above the track, which greatly reduces **friction**. When **electromagnets** in the train are switched on and off, the train moves forward or stops. Maglev is short for magnetic levitation.
The passengers travelled on the maglev train.

magnetic levitation ► **maglev train**

magnetic compass *noun*
A magnetic compass is an instrument for finding one's way. It has a **dial** containing a needle that always points to magnetic north.
Although it was foggy, they were able to find their way home by using a magnetic compass.

magnetic tape *noun*
Magnetic tape is a long ribbon of **plastic** coated with magnetic particles. **Electric signals** change the pattern of the particles on the tape. Magnetic tape is used in **tape recorders**, **video cassette recorders**, and some **computers**.
A video cassette contains magnetic tape inside a plastic case.

magnifying glass *noun*
A magnifying glass is a **device** that makes objects appear larger. It is made up of a **convex lens** in a metal or **plastic** case. It may be attached to a handle.
The print was so small that he had to use a magnifying glass to read it.

mainframe computer *noun*
A mainframe computer is the largest and most powerful kind of **computer**. It can fill a whole room. Mainframe computers are found in the offices of large companies. They can process very large amounts of **data** and do several jobs at once.
The telephone company uses a mainframe computer to work out how much customers have to pay.

manned maneuvering unit *noun*
A manned maneuvering unit, or MMU for short, is a **device** used in space exploration. It has its own air supply, and jets of compressed air blown out of a jet pack allow a MMU to move around in different directions as it floats in space.
The astronauts used a manned manoeuvring unit to explore the Moon.

measuring machines *noun*
Measuring machines are **devices** used to **calculate** measurements. **Scales**, **meters**, and **micrometers** are different kinds of measuring machines.
The weigh station has a measuring machine to weigh loaded vehicles.

mechanical *adjective*
Mechanical describes a **machine**. **Engines**, elevators, **cranes** and **bicycles** are all mechanical. They all contain moving parts that are connected together.
A mechanic is someone who has learned mechanical skills.

mechanical energy *noun*
Mechanical energy is energy that is produced by **machines**. An **engine** changes **chemical** energy in a **fuel** into mechanical energy. Mechanical energy does work by moving things. It means the same as **kinetic energy**.
A bicycle turns human energy into mechanical energy.

mechanical tunnel-borer   *noun*
A mechanical tunnel-borer is a machine for boring tunnels through rock. It works like a giant **drill**. A mechanical tunnel-borer has sharp teeth which turn, or rotate, at high speed and tear the rock away.
The mechanical tunnel-borer dug a tunnel under the mountain for a new road.

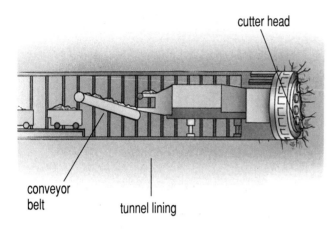

cutter head

conveyor belt

tunnel lining

medium-wave radio   *noun*
Medium-wave radio is a method of **transmitting** and **receiving** signals by **radio**. Medium-wave radio can be received several hundred miles from the **transmitter**.
Some small radios can receive programs only on medium-wave radio.

megabyte   *noun*
A megabyte, or meg for short, is a unit of measurement. It is used to measure the amount of **data** or information on a **floppy disk** or in the **memory** of a **computer**. One megabyte is the same as 1,000,000 **bytes** or 1,000 **kilobytes**.
The abbreviation for megabytes is MB.

memory   *noun*
The memory is a part of a **computer**. There are two kinds of memory. One is **random access memory** and the other is **read-only memory**. **Data** and **programs** are stored in these memories. The size of the memory is measured in **kilobytes** or **megabytes**.
A read-only memory is part of a computer's central processing unit.

metal detector   *noun*
A metal detector is a **device** for discovering metal hidden underground. It sends out **electric signals**. If they strike metal they send a sound signal back to the user.
Metal detectors are often used by treasure hunters who are looking for old coins, jewelry and other valuable objects.

meter   *noun*
A meter is a **measuring machine**. Water meters measure the flow of water. Electric meters measure the flow of **electricity**. Meters can be either **analogue** or **digital**.
She looked at the meter to see how much electricity the family had used.

microchip ► integrated circuit

microcomputer   *noun*
A microcomputer is the smallest kind of **computer**. It is sometimes called a personal computer. Microcomputers are used in many homes, schools, and offices.
She used a microcomputer to do her math homework.

micrometer   *noun*
A micrometer is a **measuring machine** that measures very small distances. The object to be measured is held between two jaws. A **scale** shows the distance between the jaws, which is the measurement of the object.
The engineer measured the thickness of the metal with a micrometer.

microphone *noun*
A microphone is a **device** used to change sound waves into **electric signals**. Microphones are used in **radio** and in **sound recording**.
There is a small microphone in the mouthpiece of a telephone.

microprocessor *noun*
A microprocessor is an **integrated circuit**. Part of a **computer**, it controls the **data** and **programs** that the computer uses. Microprocessors are also found in **digital watches**, **electronic calculators**, and some **appliances**, such as **automatic washing machines**.
The invention of the microprocessor allowed very small computers to be made.

microscope *noun*
A microscope is an instrument that can make very small objects seem much larger. An ordinary microscope contains **lenses**. An **electron microscope** uses an **electron gun** to magnify objects.
He used a microscope to study a grain of sand.

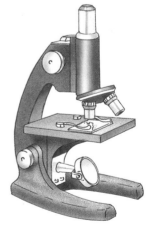

microwave oven *noun*
A microwave oven is a cooking **appliance**. Microwaves are very short **radio waves**. When they strike food, particles of the food vibrate against each other. This produces heat by **friction** and cooks the food.
A meal can be prepared very quickly using a microwave oven.

milking machine *noun*
A milking machine is a **dairy machine** used for milking cows. It **pumps** the milk away from the cow's udders to a storage container. The suction pump is driven by **electricity**.
Milking machines are found in a farm's dairy.

mincer *noun*
A mincer is an **appliance** used in cooking. It cuts food into small pieces. A mincer can be worked by hand or **powered** by an **electric motor**.
She put the meat through the mincer and then put it in the sauce.

mirror *noun*
A mirror is a **device** that reflects light. It is usually made of **glass** coated on one side with a silver substance. A mirror presents an image of objects in front of it.
Before he went out he looked at himself in the mirror.

missile *noun*
1. A missile is anything that is pushed forward by **force**. **Bullets** and artillery shells are missiles.
The crowd threw stones and other missiles at the robbers.
2. A missile is a **vehicle** that carries an explosive **warhead**. It can be fired in the air or in space. Missiles are **powered** by **rocket motors** or by **jet engines**.
The bomber was shot down by a ground-to-air missile.

model *noun*
1. A model is a small copy of something larger. Engineers often build models to help them find out how real **machines** will behave.
The engineers tested a model of the new airliner in a wind tunnel.
2. A model is a version of a machine in a slightly different form.
He exchanged his old car for this year's model.

multistage rocket *noun*

A multistage rocket is a **vehicle** used to put objects into space. It has **rocket motors** in each stage. Each motor takes the vehicle part of the way.

A multistage rocket was used to put the satellite into space.

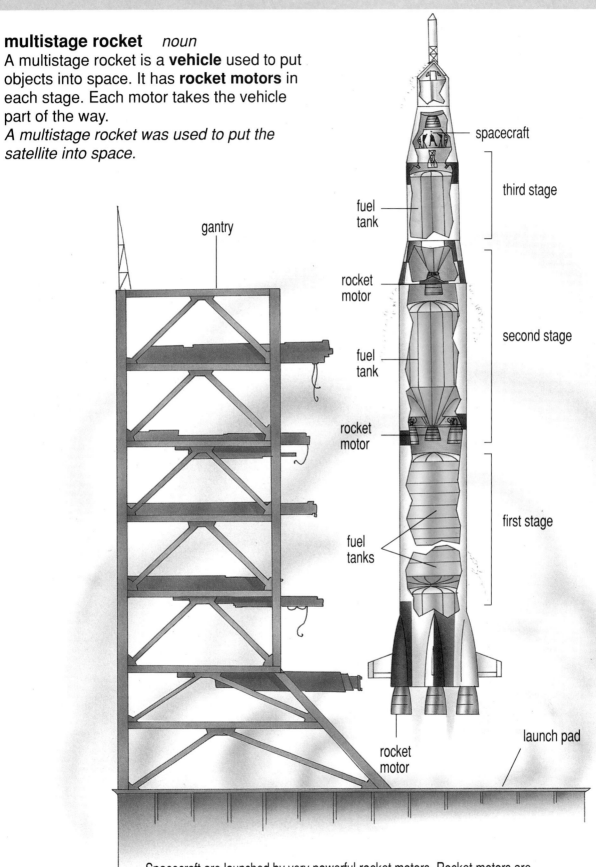

spacecraft

third stage

fuel tank

rocket motor

fuel tank

second stage

rocket motor

fuel tanks

first stage

gantry

rocket motor

launch pad

Spacecraft are launched by very powerful rocket motors. Rocket motors are similar to jet engines. They move forward by pushing out, or expelling, a powerful stream of burning gases.

86

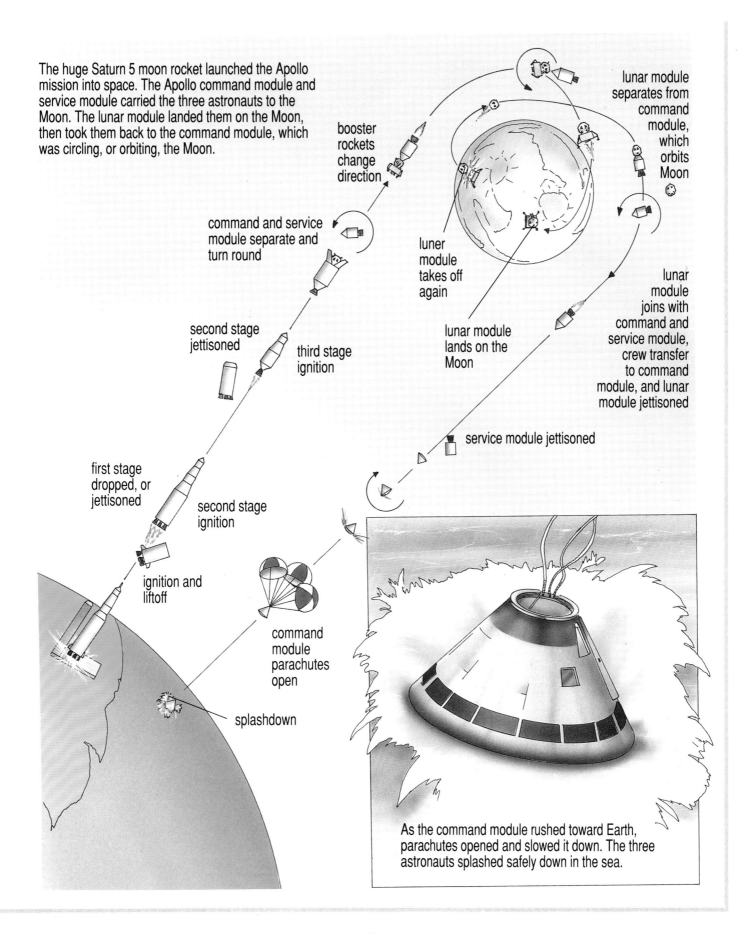

The huge Saturn 5 moon rocket launched the Apollo mission into space. The Apollo command module and service module carried the three astronauts to the Moon. The lunar module landed them on the Moon, then took them back to the command module, which was circling, or orbiting, the Moon.

lunar module separates from command module, which orbits Moon

booster rockets change direction

command and service module separate and turn round

luner module takes off again

lunar module lands on the Moon

lunar module joins with command and service module, crew transfer to command module, and lunar module jettisoned

second stage jettisoned

third stage ignition

service module jettisoned

first stage dropped, or jettisoned

second stage ignition

ignition and liftoff

command module parachutes open

splashdown

As the command module rushed toward Earth, parachutes opened and slowed it down. The three astronauts splashed safely down in the sea.

modem   *noun*
A modem is a **device** that is used with some **computers**. It connects the computer to a telephone line.
Computers with modems can send information to each other over telephone lines.

motion picture   *noun*
A motion picture is a **film** that is shown in a theater using a **movie projector**. Motion pictures are more commonly known as movies.
Many motion pictures are now available on videocassette.

motor   *noun*
A motor is a kind of **machine** that changes **chemical**, electrical or other kinds of energy into **mechanical energy**. This mechanical energy is used to do work. **Electric motors** and **automobile engines** are different kinds of motors.
The toy car was powered by a clockwork motor.

motorcycle   *noun*
A motorcycle is a two-**wheeled** road **vehicle**. It has an **internal combustion engine** that burns **gasoline**. Motorcycles can usually also carry a passenger who sits behind the driver.
He gave his brother a ride on his new motorcycle.

mouse   *noun*
A mouse is a **device** that is used with some **computers**. It is a small box with buttons on top and a ball underneath. When the mouse is moved over a surface, the ball rolls and a marker appears on the **visual display unit**. Pressing the buttons on the mouse gives instructions to the computer.
A mouse tells a computer to carry out different functions.

mouthpiece   *noun*
A mouthpiece is the part of a **telephone** into which a person speaks. A mouthpiece contains a small **microphone**, which sends **electric signals** down the telephone line.
She picked up the telephone and spoke into the mouthpiece.

movie camera   *noun*
A movie camera is a kind of **camera** that is used to make **motion pictures**. It contains an **electric motor**, which winds the film through the camera and takes thousands of **photographs** one after the other.
The movie camera began to roll and the actors started playing their parts.

movie projector   *noun*
A movie projector is a **machine** for showing **motion pictures**. It unwinds a **film** in front of a bright light. The pictures on the film are projected through **lenses** onto a screen.
He loaded a new film into the movie projector.

multistage rocket ► page 86

nail clipper *noun*
A nail clipper is a **device** for cutting finger- and toenails. It clips the ends off with a sharp blade, and works with a **lever mechanism**.
He trimmed his fingernails with a nail clipper.

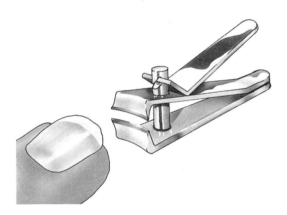

nail extractor *noun*
A nail extractor is a **device** for removing nails from wood or other materials. A claw **hammer** has a nail extractor at one end of the head. The claw is placed under the head of the nail and the handle of the hammer is used as a **lever** to pull the nail out.
Before the carpenter could start work, he had to remove all the old nails from the wood with a nail extractor.

natural gas *noun*
Natural gas is a **fossil fuel**. It is a mixture of a number of different **gases**, which burn when they are ignited. Natural gas is tapped or **pumped** from wells in the Earth. Many homes in towns and cities are connected to a natural gas supply.
Natural gas was used to heat the water and cook the food.

network *noun*
A network describes two or more **computers** that are linked so that they work together.
Computers in a network can share information and data.

neutron bomb *noun*
A neutron bomb is a powerful **nuclear weapon** known as an enhanced radiation weapon. It can kill soldiers on a battlefield, but it does little harm to nearby buildings and other property.
A neutron bomb can be dropped from an aircraft or used as the warhead of a missile.

nonreturn valve *noun*
A nonreturn valve is a **device** that allows **gas** or liquid to pass through in only one direction.
The air in the tire cannot escape because it is pumped in through a nonreturn valve.

nuclear *adjective*
Nuclear describes the breaking apart or joining together of atoms. The breaking apart of atoms is called nuclear fission. Joining atoms together is called nuclear fusion. Both these processes cause the release of nuclear energy.
Modern submarines are nuclear powered.

nuclear power station *noun*
A nuclear power station **generates electricity**. Heat from a **nuclear reactor** boils water to produce steam. The steam drives the **shaft** of a **generator**.
Nuclear power stations are often near the sea, which carries away waste water produced by the power stations.

nuclear reactor *noun*
A nuclear reactor is a **device** that uses **nuclear fuel** to release energy. The reactor in a **nuclear power station** produces heat, which boils water to make steam.
A nuclear reactor is surrounded by a thick, concrete wall.

nuclear weapon   *noun*
A nuclear weapon is a **bomb** or **missile** that contains a **nuclear warhead**. It can be dropped from an **aircraft**, fired from a **gun**, or fitted with a **rocket motor**.
Many people would like to see a worldwide ban on the making of nuclear weapons.

numerically controlled machine tool
noun
A numerically controlled machine tool is a **machine tool** that is connected to a **computer**. The computer sends instructions to the machine tool, which then performs tasks automatically. NMT is short for numerically controlled machine tools.
Most of the work in the factory was done by numerically controlled machine tools.

nut   *noun*
A nut is a fastening **device**. It is a piece of metal with four or six sides and a hole in the middle. Inside the hole is a spiral groove called a thread. This fits with the thread on a **bolt**. Nuts and bolts are used to fasten things together.
He used a wrench to tighten the nut around the bolt.

nutcracker   *noun*
A nutcracker is a **device** for breaking open the shells of nuts. It is a kind of **lever**. The fulcrum of this lever is at one end, with the **load** in the middle. The nutcracker's jaws crush the shell when the handles are squeezed together.
The nuts were so hard that it was difficult to open them even with a nutcracker.

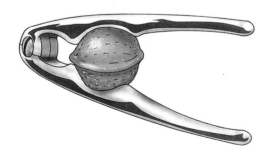

nylon   *noun*
Nylon is a kind of **plastic**. It is made from **chemicals**. Nylon fibers can be spun into cloth or ropes. Pieces of hard nylon are often used for small **machine** parts.
The outside shell of his parka was made of nylon.

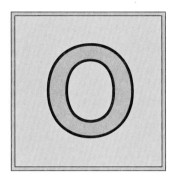

offset lithography   *noun*
Offset lithography is a kind of **lithographic printing**. The image on the lithographic plate is transferred to a roller. Then the roller is inked and pressed onto the paper.
Most newspapers are printed by offset lithography.

oil   *noun*
An oil is a kind of fatty or greasy liquid that does not mix or dissolve in water, but will dissolve in alcohol. Many oils are used as **lubricants**. When used as a lubricant a **film** of oil is spread over the moving parts of a **machine** to reduce **friction**. Most lubricating oil is made from **petroleum**, but other kinds of oil, such as castor oil, are also sometimes used as lubricants.
He put oil on his bicycle chain so that it would be easy to pedal.

oil lamp   *noun*
An oil lamp is a kind of lamp that uses **oil** as **fuel**. The oil is stored at the bottom of the lamp and soaks up a wick to the **burner**, where it is lit, or ignited.
There was no electricity in the house, so they found their way upstairs with an oil lamp.

oil pump   *noun*
An oil pump is part of many **machines**. It pumps **oil** to places in the machine where a **lubricant** is needed. Lubricants reduce **friction** and take away heat.
The oil pump in an automobile can pump oil around the moving parts of the engine.

oil refinery   *noun*
An oil refinery is a place where **petroleum** is processed into different substances. The petroleum is heated in a **furnace**. A **fractionating column** then separates the petroleum into various liquids and **gases**.
Products made at an oil refinery have many uses.

oil rig   ► page 92

oil tanker   *noun*
An oil tanker is a kind of **ship** built to carry large amounts of **oil** or oil products. Oil tankers call at special ports called **oil terminals**.
The oil tanker was carrying many thousands of tons of kerosene.

oil terminal   *noun*
An oil terminal is a port where **oil tankers** load or unload their cargoes. Oil terminals are equipped with **pumps**, storage tanks, and **pipelines**.
The oil tanker is due to sail from the oil terminal tomorrow.

ophthalmoscope   *noun*
An ophthalmoscope is an instrument used to inspect a person's eyes for disease or damage. It shines a narrow beam of light through the iris into the eyeball.
The doctor asked the girl to open her eyes while he looked at them through an ophthalmoscope.

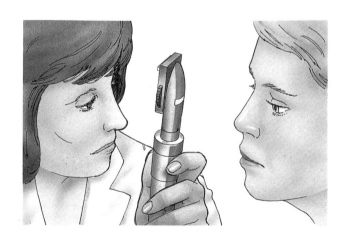

oil rig *noun*

An oil rig is a **structure** that is found at an oil well on land or at sea. It is a tower that contains a **drill**, which bores into the ground or seabed below the rig. Exploration rigs search for new supplies of oil. Production rigs pump oil to the surface.
Work on an oil rig at sea is hard and often dangerous.

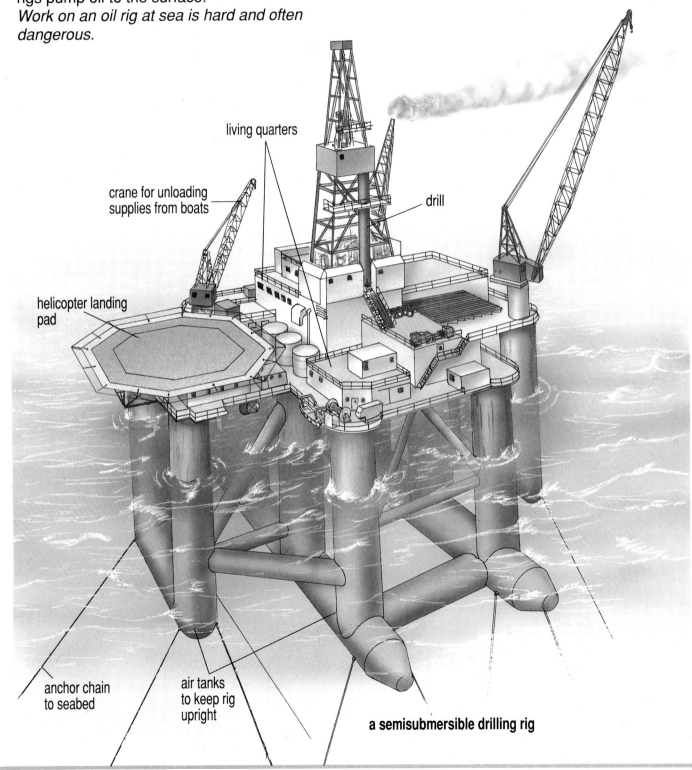

living quarters

crane for unloading supplies from boats

drill

helicopter landing pad

anchor chain to seabed

air tanks to keep rig upright

a semisubmersible drilling rig

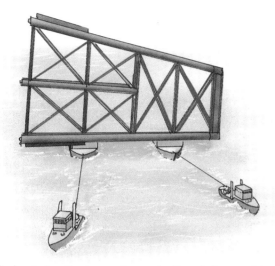

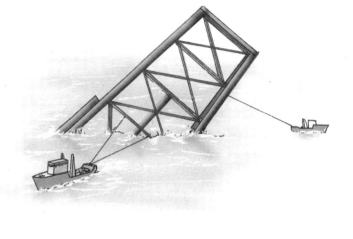

1. Tugboats tow the base of a production platform out to sea on its side.

2. The boats turn the base over and it is set upon the seabed.

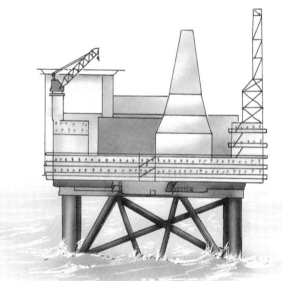

3. Decks are placed on the production platform and a crane lifts a block of buildings onto the decks.

4. The production rig is ready for work.

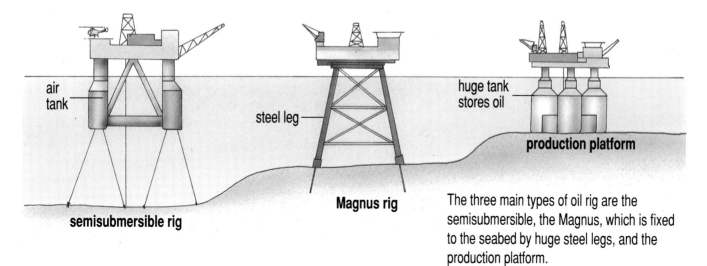

air tank

semisubmersible rig

steel leg

Magnus rig

huge tank stores oil

production platform

The three main types of oil rig are the semisubmersible, the Magnus, which is fixed to the seabed by huge steel legs, and the production platform.

optical fiber   *noun*
An optical fiber is a thin, hollow thread made from **glass**. Optical fibers are bundled together to make optical **cables**. Messages in the form of light signals are sent along optical fibers by **laser** light.
Cables made up of optical fibers can carry more messages than copper wire cables.

optical instruments   *noun*
Optical instruments are instruments that make use of light energy. They usually have **lenses** to direct the flow of light. **Telescopes** and **binoculars** are optical instruments.
Optical instruments are very carefully made to make sure they are accurate.

output   *noun*
Output is anything produced by a **machine** or other **device**. The output of a **computer** can be seen on a **screen** or printed on paper. The output from a factory is the goods it makes.
The output from a tape player is the sound that comes through the loudspeaker or earphones.

overshot waterwheel   *noun*
An overshot waterwheel is a kind of **engine** driven by water **power**. The water supply is piped so that it pours out above the waterwheel and drops onto it, making it turn around, or rotate. The rotation is used to drive **machinery**.
Power from an overshot waterwheel was once used to grind corn into flour.

pacemaker   *noun*
A pacemaker is a **device** that is fitted into the body of a person with heart disease. It is **powered** by a tiny **battery** and gives out **electric signals** that help the person's heart to beat regularly.
Her grandfather went into the hospital to get a pacemaker.

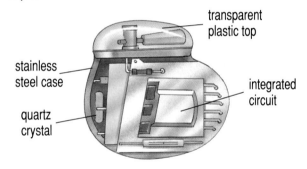

transparent plastic top

stainless steel case

quartz crystal

integrated circuit

padlock   *noun*
A padlock is a kind of **lock** used to secure objects that are not fitted with locks of their own. It has a curved bar that can be slipped through a chain or other strong fixture. Most padlocks have **keys**, but some are **combination locks**.
He secured his bicycle with a padlock so that it would not be stolen.

parachute   *noun*
A parachute is a **device** that slows down objects that are falling through air. It has a canopy made of silk or **nylon** cloth. Ropes connect the canopy to a harness. When it is not being used, a parachute is folded into a small package. When it opens, the canopy resists, or pushes against, the air flowing past it.
The pilot landed safely by parachute.

paraffin *noun*
Paraffin is a waxy substance made from **petroleum**.
Some candles are made of paraffin.

parking meter *noun*
A parking meter is a **device** that shows how long a **vehicle** has been parked in a particular space. It is operated by a coin. The coin starts a **clockwork motor**, which drives a needle, showing how much time has gone by.
He found a place to park and put some money in the parking meter.

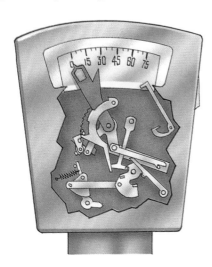

pedal-power plane *noun*
A pedal-power plane is an **aircraft** that is powered by human energy. It has pedals like a **bicycle**. Movement of the pedals makes a **propeller** turn and pull the plane through the air.
Pedal-power planes are made and flown for fun.

pedometer *noun*
A pedometer is a **device** that is carried by someone walking. The **mechanism** inside a pedometer records each step the walker takes and computes the distance traveled. A pedometer might be useful for someone who uses walking as part of an exercise program.
His pedometer showed that he had walked nearly 5 miles.

pencil sharpener *noun*
A pencil sharpener is a simple **device** for sharpening pencils. It uses a wedge with a sharp edge to shave the end of the pencil.
He sharpened the pencil to a fine point with the pencil sharpener.

pendulum clock ► page 96

pendulum seismograph *noun*
A pendulum seismograph is a **device** for recording the strength of earthquakes. It has a pendulum attached to a pen that marks paper fixed to a drum. Earthquake waves cause the drum to move, but the pendulum stays still.
The pendulum seismograph showed that the earthquake had been a severe one.

percolator *noun*
A percolator is a **device** for making coffee. Boiling water rises up a tube in the center of the percolator and drains down through a **filter** containing ground coffee.
After the meal, they had fresh coffee made with a percolator.

periscope *noun*
A periscope is a **device** that allows people to see over or around objects. It uses **mirrors** to reflect rays of light from the object to our eyes. Periscopes in **submarines** allow the crew to see above the surface of the sea.
He used a periscope to see over the wall into the garden.

personal computer ► **microcomputer**

personal stereo *noun*
A personal stereo is a small **cassette tape recorder** that can be carried in a pocket or worn on a belt. It has **earphones** so that **tapes** can be heard in private. And some personal stereos also have a **radio**. Some record sound as well as play it back.
While jogging, she listened to some music on her personal stereo.

pendulum clock   *noun*

A pendulum clock is a **clock** with a pendulum that helps it keep accurate time. A pendulum is a long rod with a weight on one end. The other end is connected to a **clockwork motor**. The pendulum swings to and fro, and the length of its swing can be adjusted to make the clock go faster or slower.

Grandfather clocks are pendulum clocks.

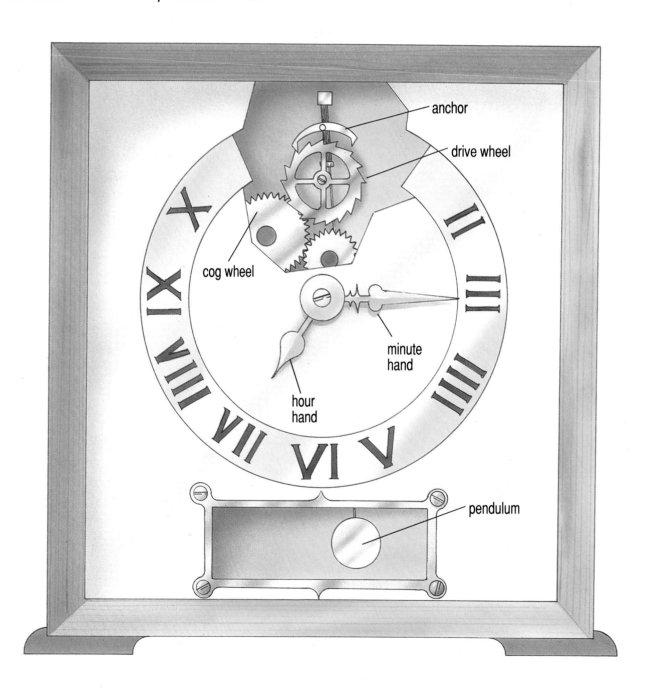

anchor

drive wheel

cog wheel

minute hand

hour hand

pendulum

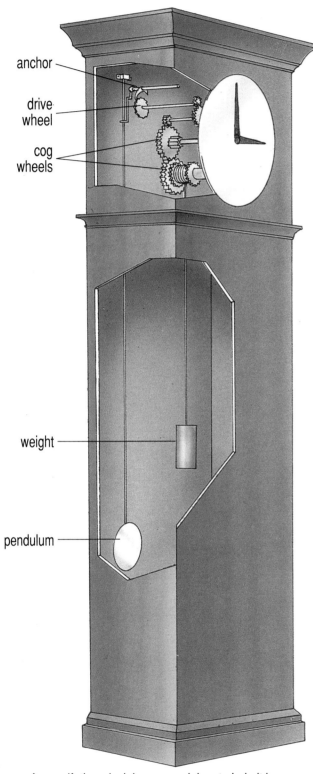

anchor

drive
wheel

cog
wheels

weight

pendulum

A grandfather clock has a pendulum to help it keep good time. As it swings, the pendulum rocks the anchor that controls the turning of the drive wheel.

escapement

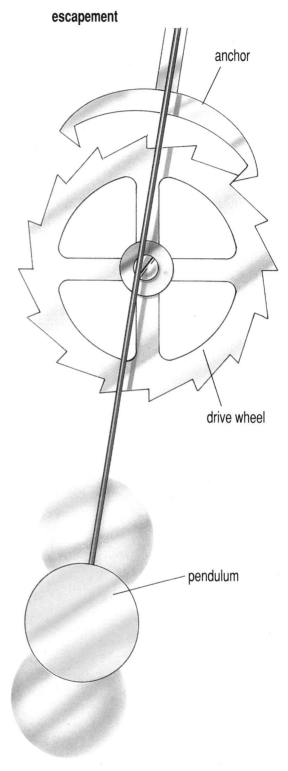

anchor

drive wheel

pendulum

The escapement makes the hands tick forward. As it rocks to one side, the anchor catches in the cogs of the drive wheel and stops it from moving. As the anchor rocks to the other side, the drive wheel is released for a short time. The weight on the drive wheel falls, turning the drive wheel and hands.

petroleum *noun*
Petroleum is a dark, oily liquid that is found beneath the surface of the Earth. It is refined at an **oil refinery** to make many different products. Another name for petroleum is crude **oil**. Much of the petroleum pumped out of the Earth is refined to make gasoline that is used to power different machines including automobiles. The gasoline is transported from the refineries to a gasoline station and is pumped into cars and trucks through a gasoline pump.
The petroleum was refined into gasoline for use in automobiles.

gasoline pump

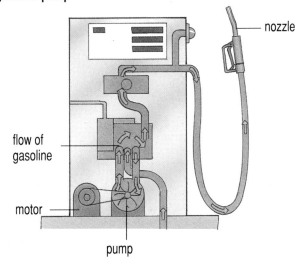

nozzle
flow of gasoline
motor
pump

photo booth *noun*
A photo booth is a cubicle that contains an automatic **camera**. It uses an **electronic flash** to take **photographs**. A person operates the camera by putting coins in a slot, then the pictures are taken.
She needed a new passport photograph, so she went to a photo booth.

photochronograph *noun*
A photochronograph is a **machine** that photographs a moving object at regular, but very small, intervals.
They used a photochronograph to photograph the action of the bird's wing.

photocopier ▶ page 100

photograph *noun*
A photograph is an image recorded on **film** by a **camera**. The film is sensitive to light. A photograph may be in color or in black and white.
On the shelf there was a photograph taken when he was two years old.

phototransistor *noun*
A phototransistor is a kind of **sensor**. It is an electrical **device** that is sensitive to light. Light falling on a phototransistor can be used to switch an **appliance** on or off. Phototransistors are used to operate automatic doors and in some **burglar alarms**.
When the car interrupted the beam of light hitting the phototransistor, the door opened.

piano *noun*
A piano is a large musical instrument. It contains strings that make musical notes when they are struck by felt **hammers**. The player presses **keys** on the piano's **keyboard** to move the hammers.
She sat at the piano and played a tune.

pig iron *noun*
Pig iron is a gray metal. It is made in a **blast furnace**. While it is still liquid, it is poured into molds to set into blocks that are called pigs. Most pig iron is used to make **steel**.
Pig iron is hard but brittle and breaks easily.

pile driver *noun*
A pile driver is a **machine** that drives metal or concrete posts into the ground. It has a very heavy **hammer** that is raised by a **crane** and then allowed to drop.
The workers used a pile driver to make the foundations of the new shopping center.

pipeline *noun*
A pipeline is a long pipe used to carry liquids or **gases** over long distances. Pipelines are usually laid underground and are made of **steel**, **plastic**, or concrete.
The pipeline carried petroleum from the oil well to the refinery.

piston *noun*
A piston is a part of a **machine** that moves backward and forward inside a **cylinder**. When vapor in the cylinder expands, it forces the piston down, producing mechanical energy. Pistons are found in **internal combustion engines**, **pumps**, and **hydraulic systems**.
The pistons in a car engine make the crankshaft rotate.

plane *noun*
1. A plane is a hand **tool**. It is used to smooth and shape wood. It is made up of a boxlike frame with a handle. The flat, metal base has a slit with a sharp blade sticking through.
As the plane moved across the wood, the blade shaves off a thin sliver of material.
2. A plane is a flat surface. An **inclined plane** is a plane that is raised at one end. It is a kind of **simple machine**.
The top of a table is a plane.

planetary gears *plural noun*
Planetary gears are **gearwheels** that are arranged in a special way. The "planet" **wheels** move round a central "sun" wheel. They take their name from the way the planets move round the sun.
Planetary gears are found in cars with automatic transmissions.

plastic *noun*
Plastic is an artificial material that can be molded into different shapes. It is made by mixing **chemicals**. **Nylon** is one type of plastic.
The kitchen table had a top made of plastic.
plastic *adjective*

platform scale *noun*
A platform scale is a **weighing machine**. The object to be weighed is placed on a platform. The weight is shown in ounces and pounds on a kind of **meter**.
Bathroom scales are one kind of platform scale.

pliers *plural noun*
Pliers are small **tools** that grasp objects between two claws. They are often used to hold hot metal while it is being worked on. They are a simple **lever**.
The blacksmith held the horseshoe with a pair of pliers.

plow *noun*
A plow is a **machine** that digs land to prepare it for planting. It has a blade that digs into the soil and turns it over. Some plows have one row of blades, others have more. Plows are usually pulled by **tractors**.
There were deep furrows in the field where the plow had been.
plow *verb*

photocopier *noun*
A photocopier is an **appliance** that makes copies of books or sheets of paper. It works by using **static electricity** or **chemicals**. A photocopier produces copies that look exactly the same as the original.
She used a photocopier to make several copies of her poem.

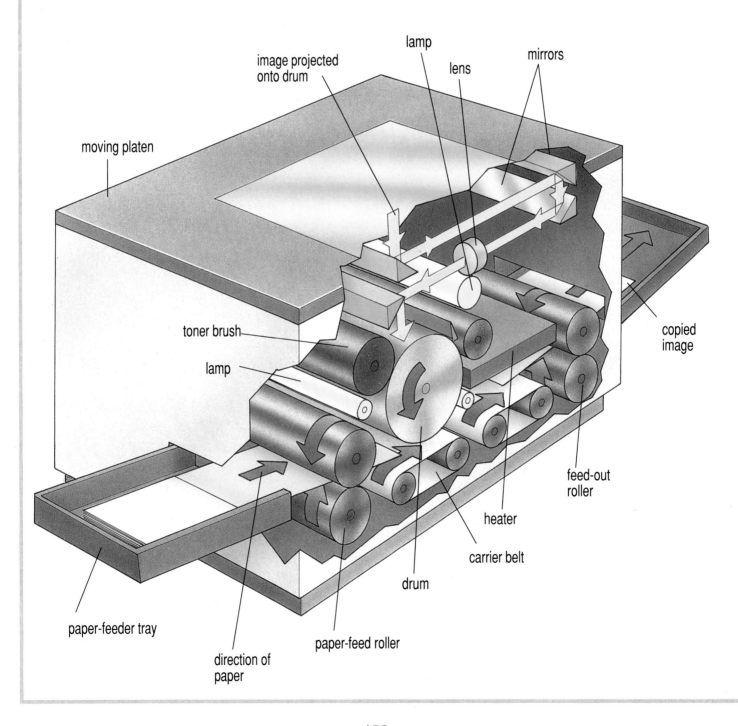

moving platen

image projected onto drum

lamp

lens

mirrors

toner brush

lamp

copied image

feed-out roller

heater

carrier belt

drum

paper-feeder tray

direction of paper

paper-feed roller

The photocopying process

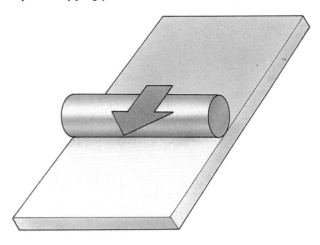

1. Electricity flows through the metal plate or cylinder and charges it.

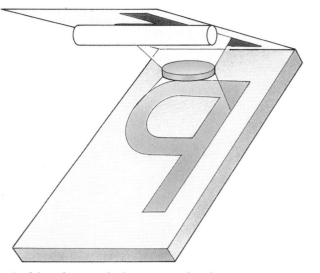

2. A lens focuses the image onto the plate.

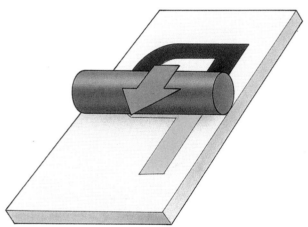

3. Toning powder is brushed over the plate and sticks to the image.

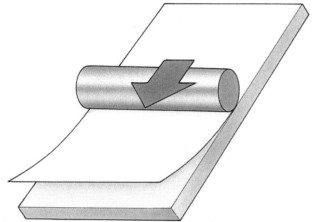

4. A piece of paper is pressed onto the plate.

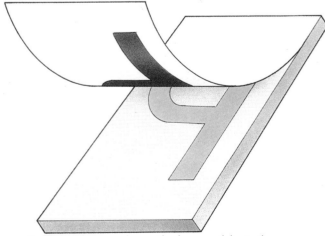

5. The toning powder on the image sticks to the paper.

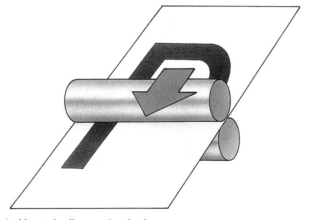

6. Heated rollers make the image permanent.

pneumatic   *adjective*
Pneumatic describes a **device** that is **powered** by **compressed air**. An **air hammer** is a pneumatic device.
Pneumatic machines are often used to build and repair roads.

pneumatic drill   *noun*
A pneumatic drill is a **tool** that is used for making holes in the ground. It is driven by **compressed air**.
The workman used a pneumatic drill to make a hole in the pavement for the new road sign.

pneumatic machine   *noun*
A pneumatic machine is a machine that is driven by **compressed air**. The compressed air is supplied by another **machine**, which is called a **compressor**.
The car mechanic used a pneumatic machine to polish the car's new paint.

pneumatic tire   *noun*
A pneumatic tire is a kind of **tire** that is filled with **compressed air**. Pneumatic tires are fitted to many kinds of vehicles. The air supports the weight of a vehicle and absorbs the shock of bumps in the road.
The truck had huge pneumatic tires.

pocketknife   *noun*
A pocketknife is a small knife with blades that fold into the handle, so the knife can be carried about safely. Besides the main blade, many pocketknives also have other blades, such as screwdrivers, nail files, and even miniature scissors.
He used his pocketknife to whittle the stick.

points   *plural noun*
Points are part of the **ignition system** of an **internal combustion engine**. They control the flow of **electricity** to the **spark plugs**. Many new cars are fitted with **electronic** ignitions, which do not need points.
The car is not running well because the points are dirty.

potential energy   *noun*
Potential energy is stored **energy**. Nuclear energy and chemical energy are kinds of potential energy. When an object is lifted above the ground, it stores potential energy. This energy becomes **kinetic energy** when the object falls back to the ground.
A drawn bowstring stores potential energy.

potter's wheel   *noun*
A potter's wheel is a **machine** for making round, **cylindrical** objects out of clay. A ball of clay is placed on the **wheel**. As the wheel **rotates**, the potter shapes the clay by hand. A potter's wheel is driven by a **treadle** or by an **electric motor**.
We learned how to make a jug on the potter's wheel.

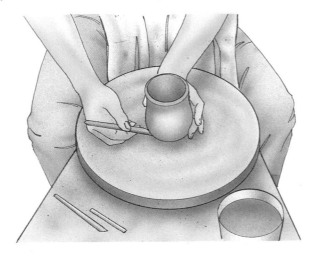

power   *noun*
Power is the amount of work done in a certain length of time. The power of an **engine** is the greatest amount of work it can do to drive a **machine**. The power of a **light bulb** is the amount of light it gives out and how much **electricity** it uses. In the metric system power is measured in watts. But because a watt is a very small unit, we generally use kilowatts, which are equal to 1,000 watts. The power of a car is measured in **horsepower**. Each horsepower equals .746 kilowatts.
His new motorcycle has twice as much power as his old scooter.
power   *verb*

power boat   *noun*

A power boat is a **boat** with an **engine**. The engine is mounted at the rear of the boat and is generally powered by **gasoline**. Different kinds of power boats are used for pleasure and for racing in competitions around the world.

The power boat flashed past with a roar.

power drill   *noun*

A power drill is a **drill** driven by an **electric motor**. It is used to make small, round holes in hard surfaces.

He used a power drill to make a hole in the wall.

power station   *noun*

A power station is a place where **electricity** is made. In large power stations, **fuel** is burned to boil water and make steam. The steam spins a **turbine**, which drives a **generator**.

A train carried coal to the power station for use in its boilers.

power takeoff   *noun*

Power takeoff is a **device**, usually found on a **tractor** or truck, that allows the **power** of the **engine** to be used to run another piece of equipment. Tow trucks use power takeoff to operate their hook, and tractors use power takeoff to operate pieces of farm **machinery**.

The farmer baled the straw with a baler driven by a power takeoff.

pressure gauge   *noun*

A pressure gauge is an instrument that measures the **force** of a **gas** or liquid. One kind of gauge is used to test the pressure of air inside **tires** of road **vehicles**. The pressure of the air is shown on a **scale** or a **meter**.

She used a pressure gauge to check whether her bicycle tires had enough air in them.

printer   *noun*

A printer is the part of a **computer** or **word processor** that prints the **output** from the computer or word processor on paper using a **print head**. The main kinds of printer are **daisy wheel**, **dot matrix**, **bubblejet**, and **laser**.

Some printers can produce drawings or diagrams in different colors.

print head   *noun*

A print head is the part of a **printer** that makes marks on the paper. The print head of a **daisy wheel printer** is a wheel with a number or letter on each spoke.

He cleaned the print head of the bubblejet printer because the holes were clogged.

printing press ► page 104

processing unit ► **central processing unit**

processor ► **microprocessor**

product   *noun*

A product is something that has been made. It is usually something that is made up of smaller parts. A product may be food or clothing, a **device** or an **appliance**. Most products are made in factories. Some products are put together, or assembled, piece by piece, on an **assembly line** by **machines**. Other products are assembled by hand.

The factory made plastics into many different products.

printing press *noun*

A printing press is a **machine** that is used to print on paper. Some presses print on paper cut into sheets. Others print on paper from large rolls. **Letterpress** presses and **offset lithography** presses are two kinds of printing press.

They saw the first copies of the newspaper come off the printing press.

In offset lithography, a flat plate is treated, or etched, so that only the areas to be printed attract a greasy ink.

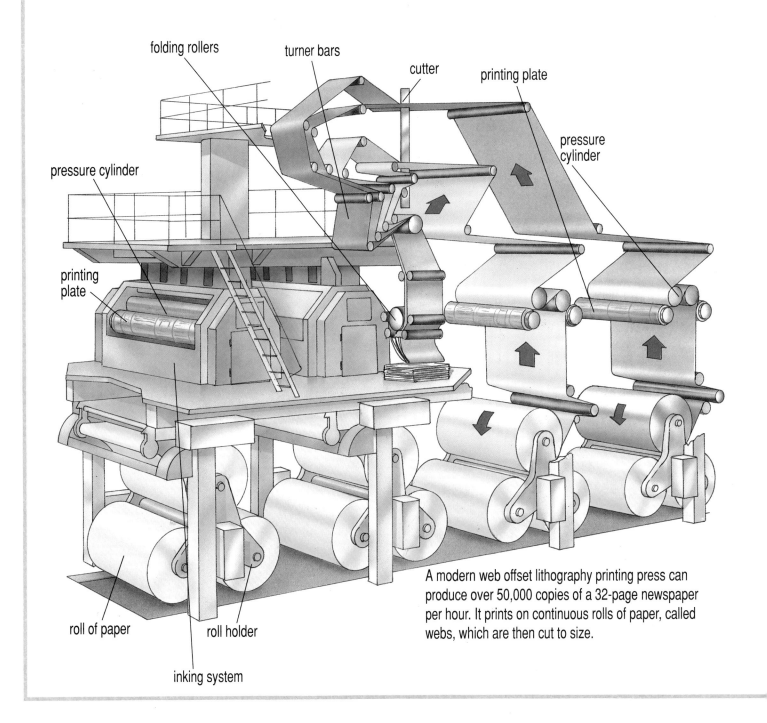

folding rollers

turner bars

cutter

printing plate

pressure cylinder

pressure cylinder

printing plate

roll of paper

roll holder

inking system

A modern web offset lithography printing press can produce over 50,000 copies of a 32-page newspaper per hour. It prints on continuous rolls of paper, called webs, which are then cut to size.

Methods of printing

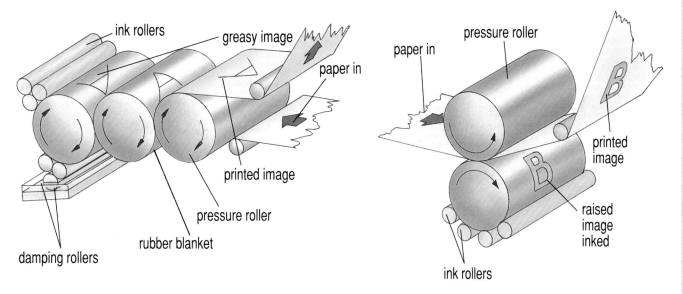

1. Offset lithography uses a flat plate that is treated to receive ink only on the areas to be printed. The inked image is transferred onto a rubber blanket which presses it onto the paper.

2. In letterpress printing, the image is a raised area on the plate. Only this raised area receives ink.

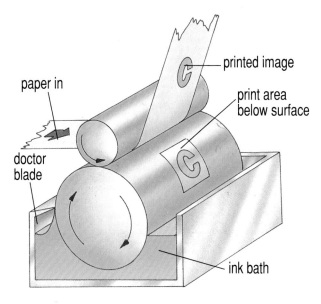

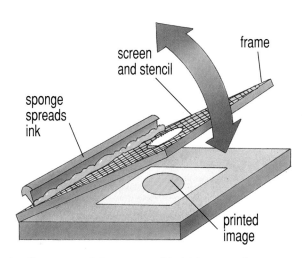

3. In gravure printing, the image is cut into the plate. The whole surface is inked. A doctor blade scrapes ink off the raised part, leaving only the image filled with ink.

4. In silk-screen printing, a stencil is laid on top of a screen made from very fine net. Ink is forced through the screen onto the paper and the stencil forms the image.

program *noun*
A program is a set of instructions that is loaded into a **computer**. It tells the computer how to perform different tasks. Programs are stored on **floppy disks**, **hard disks**, or **magnetic tape**.
He used a floppy disk to load a new program into his computer.

projector *noun*
A projector is a **device** that throws an image through **lenses** onto a screen. The image is thrown by a bright **light bulb**. **Slide projectors** and **movie projectors** are two kinds of projector.
He put a reel of film in the projector and started the movie.

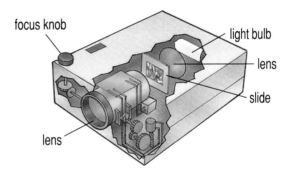

propeller *noun*
A propeller is a part of a **ship** and of some **airplanes**. It has two or more curved blades fixed to a **shaft**. The shaft is turned by an **engine**. As the propeller blades **rotate**, a **force** pushes or pulls the ship or airplane forward.
The propellers of a ship cannot usually be seen because they are under water.

pulley *noun*
A pulley is a **simple machine**. It is a wheel with a groove around the edge and a rope or **cable** in this groove. Pulling on the rope or cable allows a weight on the other end to be lifted. Heavier loads can be lifted by using more than one pulley wheel for the same rope.
The mechanic lifted the engine out of the car by using a pulley.

pump *noun*
A pump is a **device** for moving liquids or **gases** from one place to another. The pump in a central heating system moves hot water through the pipes. **Centrifugal pumps** and **reciprocating pumps** are two kinds of pump.
She used a pump to fill her bicycle tires with air.

pump *verb*

quantum mechanics   *plural noun*
Quantum mechanics is a theory about the behavior of certain kinds of energy, which are made up of small bursts or waves. Each burst is called a quantum. Light is one of the kinds of energy that behaves in this way.
The theory of quantum mechanics explains why light waves can be changed into small electric currents.

quartz clock   *noun*
A quartz clock is a kind of **clock** that contains a crystal of a mineral called quartz. An **electric current** makes the quartz move backward and forward very quickly, or vibrate. The vibrations drive a small **motor**.
Quartz clocks keep very accurate time.

rack-and-pinion gears   *plural noun*
Rack-and-pinion gears are used in the **steering** system of many cars. The pinion is a toothed **gearwheel** at the end of the steering column. It joins, or meshes, with the rack, which is a long, toothed rod. When the steering wheel is turned, rack-and-pinion gears change the turning, or **rotary**, movement into a push-and-pull movement.
Rack-and-pinion gears are connected to the front wheels of a car.

radar   *noun*
Radar is a system for finding the position of objects. A radar set sends out **radio waves**. These are bounced back, or reflected, by certain objects and show up on the **screen** of the radar set. Radar is used by **ships** and **aircraft** to check their positions.
The screen of the radar set showed that the airplane was 10 miles from the airport.

radar gun   *noun*
A radar gun is a **device** for checking the speed of moving objects. It measures speed by using **radar** and displays it on a small **screen**.
The police officer used a radar gun to check the speed of passing vehicles.

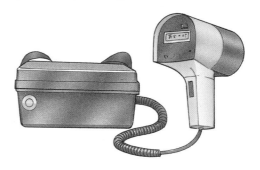

radiator *noun*

A radiator is an **appliance** that gives off heat. In a central heating system, radiators are supplied with hot water from a boiler. The heat spreads out, or radiates, through a room. Some radiators are filled with **oil**, which is heated by **electricity**.
The radiator on a car gives off heat in order to cool the engine.

radioactivity *noun*

Radioactivity is a type of **energy**. It is given off by certain elements in the form of alpha particles, beta particles and gamma rays. Elements such as radium and uranium give off radioactivity.
Radioactivity may be harmful to living things.
radioactive *adjective*

radio *noun*

1. Radio is a means of **electronic** communication. It makes use of **radio waves** to send and receive signals.
The ship's captain used his radio to call for help.
2. A radio is an electronic **device** that receives radio signals and converts them into sounds.
She switched on her radio to hear the latest news.

radio dish *noun*

A radio dish is a kind of **aerial** shaped like a shallow bowl. A radio dish collects radio signals and passes them to a **radio receiver**. A radio dish is sometimes called a satellite dish.
A radio dish may be used to communicate with satellites and spacecraft when they are travelling in space.

radio receiver *noun*

A radio receiver is an **appliance** for receiving **radio** signals. It picks up the signals from the **transmitter** and changes them into sounds.
He listened to the concert on his radio receiver.

radio station *noun*

A radio station is a place where all the equipment needed for radio broadcasting is found. It includes **radio transmitters**, **radio receivers** and broadcasting studios.
He was a broadcaster at the radio station.

radio telescope *noun*

A radio telescope is a large instrument that is used to study objects in space. It receives **radio** signals from stars and other objects. One kind of radio telescope receives signals by means of a large **radio dish**. This can be moved around to make the signals clearer.
The dish on the radio telescope was moved to make the signal clearer.

radio transmitter *noun*

A radio transmitter is an **electronic device** that sends out **radio** signals through an **aerial**. These signals can be received by **radio receivers** a long way away.
The engineer switched on the radio transmitter to start broadcasting at the beginning of the day.

radio wave *noun*

A radio wave is a kind of energy that moves through air and space. It can be made to carry messages by adding **electric signals** to it. These signals are sent out by **radio transmitters** and can be heard on **radio receivers**.
Radio waves travel at a speed of 180,000 miles per second.

raft *noun*
A raft is a simple boat with a flat bottom. Some rafts are just a platform with no sides. Others are filled with air. A raft can have a sail or be pushed along by oars or a pole.
They crossed the river on a raft they had built out of wood.

rally car *noun*
A rally car is an **automobile** that takes part in contests called rallies. It is an ordinary automobile fitted with special equipment. In rally driving, the driver must complete a set distance in a certain amount of time.
He spent many days preparing his rally car for the journey across the Sahara desert in Africa.

RAM ► **random access memory**

ramp *noun*
A ramp is an **inclined plane** that usually connects two different levels.
Ramps can be used to help people enter vehicles or buildings where steps cannot be used.

random access memory *noun*
A random access memory is the part of a **computer** that stores **programs** and **data** while the user is working on them. Random access memory, or RAM for short, is made up of **integrated cicuits**.
Information can be fed into the random access memory with the use of an input device.

ratchet *noun*
A ratchet is a kind of **gear** found in some **tools** and **machines**. It is a **wheel** or rod with teeth on its edge. The end of a **lever** joins, or meshes, with the teeth and allows the ratchet to move in only one direction.
He used a ratchet screwdriver to save time putting up the shelf.

raw material *noun*
Raw material is a natural substance used to make things. Sheep's wool is the raw material used by **spinning machines** to make wool yarn. **Iron** ore is the raw material used to make **steel**. Factories turn raw material into **products**.
Petroleum is the raw material from which petrochemicals and fuels are made.

reactor ► **nuclear reactor**

read-only memory *noun*
A read-only memory is the part of a **computer** that contains instructions that tell the computer how to do its work. It is made up of **integrated circuits**.
No data can be added to a computer's read-only memory.

rear-wheel drive *noun*
Rear-wheel drive is a system in which the engine is connected to the rear **wheels** of a **vehicle**. Many **automobiles** have rear-wheel drive.
Cars that don't have rear-wheel drive have either front-wheel drive or four-wheel drive.

receiver *noun*
1. A receiver is a **device** for receiving **electronic signals** and changing them into sounds or pictures. **Radios, televisions,** and **radar** have receivers.
He listened to music on his radio receiver.
2. A receiver is the part of a **telephone** that is held to the ear. It receives **electric signals** from the telephone line and changes them into sounds.
He put the receiver to his ear to hear what his brother was saying.
receive *verb*

reciprocating pump *noun*
A reciprocating pump is a kind of **pump** that moves a liquid or a **gas** by using a **piston**. When the piston moves in one direction, it allows the liquid or gas to enter the **cylinder**. A **bicycle** pump is a reciprocating pump.
When the piston moves in the opposite direction, it pumps the liquid or gas out of the cylinder.

record player *noun*
A record player is an **appliance** that changes vibrations into **electric signals** and changes the signals into sounds. The sounds come out of a **loudspeaker**. A record player contains a **motor** that spins records. It also has a pick-up, which collects the electric signals.
Record players play records made of vinyl.

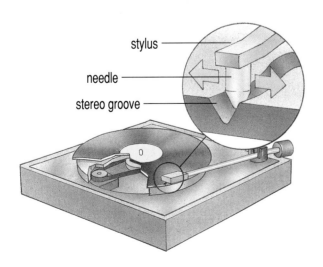

stylus

needle

stereo groove

recycle ► reprocessing

refine *verb*
Refine means to make something purer. In an **oil refinery**, pure **products** are refined from **crude oil**. During refining, mixtures are separated and impure substances are removed.
White sugar is refined from sugar cane or sugar beet so that it is pure.
refinery *noun*
refining *noun*

reflecting telescope *noun*
A reflecting telescope is an **optical instrument** for studying the night sky. Objects in the sky are reflected in one or more **mirrors**, and viewed through a **lens**.
He used a reflecting telescope to look at the planet Mars.

refractor telescope *noun*
A refractor telescope is an **optical instrument** for studying the night sky. Objects in the sky are viewed through two or more **lenses**. Refractor telescopes do not contain **mirrors**.
The boy could see many interesting things in the night sky with his refractor telescope.

refrigerator *noun*
A refrigerator is an **appliance** for keeping things cool. It contains a **pump** that circulates a **coolant** along pipes. Heat is transferred from inside the refrigerator to the coolant and given off into the room outside.
Refrigerators keep food from spoiling.
refrigerate *verb*

relay *noun*
A relay is a kind of switch that is used in many electrical **devices**. A small **electric current** flows through a device called an **electromagnet**. This makes an electric contact that switches an **electric circuit** on or off.
A relay can be used to switch an appliance on or off from a distance.

remote-control unit   *noun*
A remote-control unit is a **device** that controls a **machine** or an **electric circuit** from a distance. Many remote-control units use **radio waves** to send signals to a **receiver** inside the machine or **circuit**. Others may use a **phototransistor**.
He guided the model airplane with a remote-control unit.

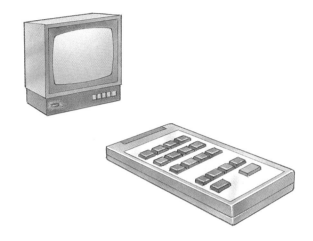

reprocessing   *noun*
1. Reprocessing is the **refining** of impure substances into pure ones. **Chemicals** that have been mixed can sometimes be reprocessed to separate the different substances they contain.
Used nuclear fuel can be changed into pure plutonium by reprocessing.
2. Reprocessing is the reusing of material that has already been used once. Reprocessing can turn old jars and bottles from a recycling center into new **glass** objects.
Old newspapers can be cleaned and turned into fresh, white paper by reprocessing.
reprocess   *verb*

rescue vehicle   *noun*
A rescue vehicle is a **vehicle** that is used to save trapped or injured people at accident sites. **Helicopters** are often used as rescue vehicles.
They placed the injured boy into the rescue vehicle and began to treat him on the way to the hospital.

resonator   *noun*
A resonator is a **device** that makes sounds louder. It **receives** the vibrations of sound waves and makes them larger.
The paper, plastic, or metal cone of a loudspeaker is a resonator.

rev counter ► **revolution counter**

revolution counter   *noun*
A revolution counter is a **device** that counts the number of revolutions made by a part of an **engine**, such as a **crankshaft**. It shows the speed at which the engine is working. Some cars are fitted with a revolution counter.
A revolution counter on a tape recorder shows how many times the reel of tape has turned.

rivet   *noun*
A rivet is a **device** for fastening two pieces of metal together. It is fixed in place with a **hammer** or a rivet gun. It does the job of a **nut** and **bolt**.
He fixed the license plate to his car with rivets.

robot   *noun*
A robot is a kind of **machine** that can do work without human help. Robots are used in many different kinds of factories. They are also used to do work that is too dangerous for human beings to perform.
Some robots are designed to work under water.

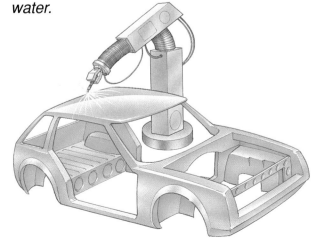

rocket *noun*
A rocket is a **device** that is **powered** by a
gas that it shoots out at high pressure. The
gas is produced by the burning of **fuel**. The
fuel used in fireworks rockets is gunpowder.
Space rockets use mixtures of solids,
liquids, or gases as fuel.
Powerful rockets sent the spacecraft into
orbit.

rocket launcher *noun*
A rocket launcher is a device for launching
rockets. Most rocket launchers are mounted
onto land vehicles, ships, or airplanes.
However, some rocket launchers are
hand-held.
The rocket sat on the rocket launcher, ready
for blastoff.

rocket motor *noun*
A rocket motor is an **engine** that works by
burning **fuel** and pushing out, or expelling,
gases at high pressure. **Spacecraft** are
powered by rocket motors. Rocket motors
contain **pumps** and other **devices** to control
the burning of the fuel.
Rocket motors are the most powerful types
of engines ever built.

rocketry *noun*
Rocketry is the science of designing,
building, and launching rockets. Rocketry
started 700 years ago, but it has only been in
the past 50 years that rockets have been
built powerful enough to launch satellites and
other spaceships into orbit around the Earth.
Robert Goddard is a major figure in the
history of rocketry.

rod thermostat *noun*
A rod thermostat is a **device** that controls
the temperature of a liquid. It is fitted inside
a **boiler** and can be set to switch off the heat
when the liquid reaches a certain
temperature. It contains a switch that is
sensitive to heat.
She set the rod thermostat on the boiler so
that the bath water would not be too hot.

roller *noun*
A roller is an object that rolls. A roller may be
made of stone, metal, wood, or **plastic**. It
can be used for pressing, crushing, or
smoothing. Heavy rollers may be used for
making or repairing roads or smoothing
down grass.
Many lawn mowers have rollers attached.

roller coaster *noun*
A roller coaster is a kind of ride found at an
amusement park. It has cars that travel
along a **track** at high speed, pulled by
gravity. The track goes up and down and
around bends to make the ride more
exciting.
She enjoyed the ride on the roller coaster,
but she was screaming all the time.

ROM ▶ **read-only memory**

rotary *adjective*
Rotary describes the circular action of part of
a **machine**. A rotary **lawn mower** has a
blade that moves in a circle, or rotates, flat
to the ground. Rotary blades, found on
helicopters, rotate fast enought to allow the
helicopter to lift off the ground. The blades
on **windmills** also have a rotary action.
The turntable of a record player moves in a
rotary motion.
rotate *verb*

rotary bit   *noun*

A rotary bit is the part of a **drill** that bores round holes as the drill is turned. It is made up of a hard-ended **steel** rod with a deep, double spiral cut down its length. The edge of the spiral is very sharp.
He made a hole in the door with a rotary bit.

rotary engine   *noun*

A rotary engine is a kind of **internal combustion engine**. It has a central part called a rotor, instead of **pistons** in **cylinders**. The rotor is made to spin around by the **force** of burning **gases**. Rotary engines have fewer moving parts than other types of internal combustion engines.
Rotary engines are sometimes used in cars.

rotary pump   *noun*

A rotary pump is a kind of **pump** that contains **gearwheels**. Liquids are forced between the teeth of the gearwheels and through the rotary pump as the wheels turn.
Rotary pumps are used to pump thick liquids, such as heavy oil.

rotary vane pump   *noun*

A rotary vane pump is a kind of **pump** that contains vanes like the blades of a **fan**. The vanes are attached to a **shaft**. When the shaft turns around, or **rotates**, the vanes move around and push liquid in front of them.
The shaft of a rotary vane pump can be driven by a gasoline, diesel, or electric motor.

rotor blades   *plural noun*

Rotor blades are the parts of a **helicopter** that hold the helicopter up in the air and control its takeoff and landing. Rotor blades are mounted above the **fuselage** of the helicopter and are driven around by the **engine**. They are sometimes known as a rotary wing.
The rotor blades began to turn, and soon the helicopter took off.

rudder   *noun*

A rudder is a **steering device** in a **ship** or an **aircraft**. It is a piece of metal that can be turned to the left or right. The ship or aircraft turns in the direction in which the rudder is moved. In a ship, the rudder is under water.
The ship's rudder moved to the right, and the ship steered right.

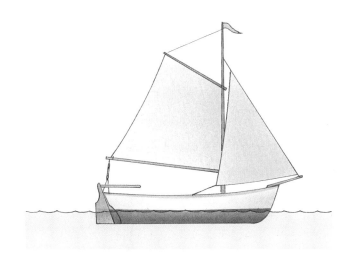

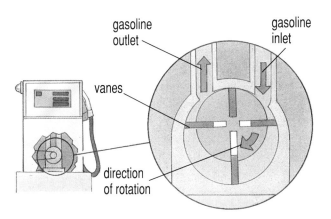

gasoline outlet
gasoline inlet
vanes
direction of rotation

safety valve   *noun*
A safety valve is a **device** for releasing pressure in a **machine**. If too much steam is present inside a **boiler**, the safety valve opens to let some of the steam out. Otherwise, the boiler might explode.
A safety valve is designed to work when pressure reaches a certain point.

satellite ▶ page 115

satellite dish   *noun*
A satellite dish is an **aerial**. It collects **radio** or **television** signals that have been sent to a **satellite** and are then bounced back to Earth. A satellite dish has to be positioned carefully to point at the satellite.
Signals from a satellite dish travel down wires to a television set.

saw   *noun*
A saw is a **device** used for cutting solid materials, such as wood or metal. It is made up of a blade with triangular teeth cut into one edge, and has a handle at one end. Some saws have their teeth bent slightly to left and right, or offset, so they do not stick in the saw cut.
He cut the wood for the fire with a saw.

scale   *noun*
A scale is a set of marks that shows a measurement. A scale is found on **meters** and some other instruments.
The scale of a barometer is marked in millibars.

scales ▶ **weighing machine**

scanner   *noun*
A scanner is a **machine** that looks at, or examines, objects. Part of the scanner moves backward, forward and downward over the object and collects information. This information forms an **electronic** picture.
A scanner inside a television camera collects information about the scene in front of it.
scan   *verb*

scissors   *plural noun*
Scissors are a **device** for cutting. They are a kind of **lever**. They squeeze the material to be cut between two sharp blades.
The hairdresser trimmed her hair with scissors.

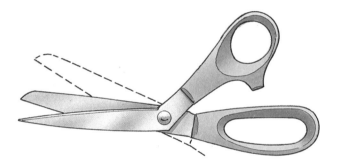

scrambler   *noun*
A scrambler is a **device** for keeping messages secret. A scrambler jumbles **electric signals** so that they can be understood only by someone who has a similar device.
The President used a scrambler to talk by telephone to his generals.
scramble   *verb*

screen   *noun*
A screen is the part of a **television** or a **visual display unit** that displays pictures or writing. A screen is made of **glass**. On the inside, it has a coating of **chemicals** that light up when hit by the beam from an **electron gun**. This forms the image that appears on the screen.
She looked at the screen of her visual display unit to see what she had written.

satellite *noun*

A satellite is an object launched into space by a **rocket**. Satellites circle, or orbit, Earth or another body in space. Earth satellites are used to observe and forecast the weather and for **telecommunications**.

The weather satellite showed that there were thunderstorms approaching.

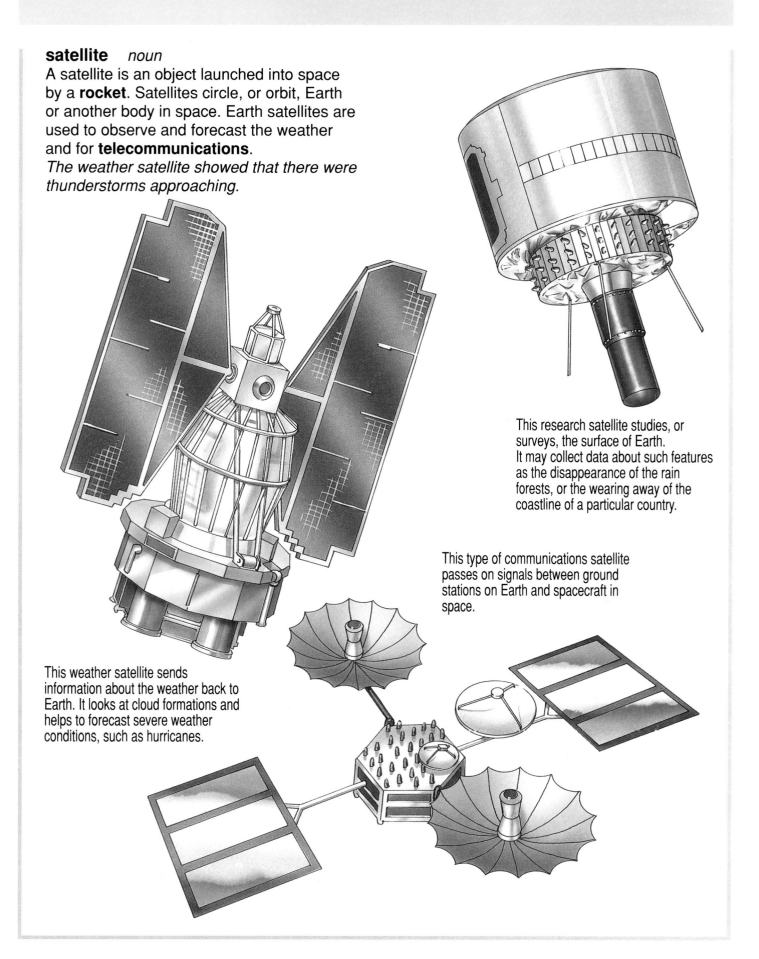

This research satellite studies, or surveys, the surface of Earth. It may collect data about such features as the disappearance of the rain forests, or the wearing away of the coastline of a particular country.

This type of communications satellite passes on signals between ground stations on Earth and spacecraft in space.

This weather satellite sends information about the weather back to Earth. It looks at cloud formations and helps to forecast severe weather conditions, such as hurricanes.

screw *noun*

A screw is a fastening **device**. It has a wide top, called the head, and a sharp, pointed end. A spiral groove called the thread runs around the body of the screw. There is a slot or a cross on the head, where the end of a **screwdriver** fits.
He used a screw to attach the mirror to the wall.
screw *verb*

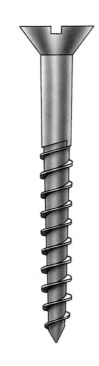

screwdriver *noun*

A screwdriver is a small **tool** used to drive **screws** into wood, metal, or other material. The head has a flat blade or a cross-shaped blade that matches the slot or the cross cut into the head of the screw. When the handle of the screwdriver is turned, the screw is driven in or twisted out.
It was impossible to undo the screw because the head of the screwdriver was not small enough to fit the screw.

screw jack *noun*

A screw jack is a lifting **device**. It is worked by turning or pulling a handle. The jack has a platform that has to be placed under the object to be lifted. When the handle of the jack is moved, the platform rises on a column that has a thread or **screw** running around it.
He used a screw jack to lift the car.

seed drill *noun*

A seed drill is a farm **machine** for planting seeds. It has a container for the seeds and releases them slowly as it is pulled over a field by a **tractor**.
The farmer brought out his seed drill to plant the barley seeds.

seismograph *noun*

A seismograph is an instrument for measuring movements of the Earth's surface. It is used to record earthquakes. **Pendulum seismographs** measure movements between a pendulum and a fixed drum and record them on paper. **Electronic** seismographs display movements on a **screen**.
The seismograph recorded a small earthquake.

semiconductor *noun*

A semiconductor is a kind of material that conducts **electricity** at a certain rate. Most semiconductors are made from silicon. Semiconductors are used in many kinds of **electronic** equipment.
A computer is able to work faster with the help of semiconductors.

sensors and detectors ▶ page 118

sewing machine *noun*

A sewing machine is a machine that automatically makes stitches in cloth. It is worked by a handle, a **treadle**, or an **electric motor**. Most sewing machines can make different kinds of stitches for different purposes.
She sat at her sewing machine and made her new dress.

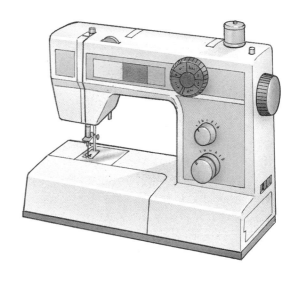

shadoof *noun*

A shadoof is a **simple machine** for raising water. It is a pole with a bucket and a **counterweight**. A shadoof is a kind of **lever**. It is used to water, or irrigate, fields in some hot countries.
The farmer raised water for his crops from the river with a shadoof.

shaft *noun*

1. A shaft is part of a **machine**. It is a rod that turns, or **rotates**, and is connected to a **wheel** or a **gear**.
Engines, motors, turbines, and propellers have shafts.
2. A shaft is a vertical tunnel. Shafts in **coal** mines carry miners and coal between the coal face and the surface. An elevator runs up and down inside a mine shaft.
A special elevator called a cage carries miners up and down the mine shaft.

shaver *noun*

A shaver is a **device** for removing hair. It has sharp blades that vibrate or **rotate** behind a grill or metal foil. A shaver is driven by a small **electric motor**.
Her father shaves every morning with an electric shaver.

sheet feeder *noun*

A sheet feeder is a **device** that puts one sheet of paper at a time into a printing **machine**. It picks the sheets up and passes them through rollers into the machine.
A printer with a sheet feeder can be left to work by itself until printing is finished.

ship ▶ page 120

shock absorber *noun*

A shock absorber is part of a **vehicle**. It has **coil springs** or a **hydraulic system** that takes in, or absorbs, the shock of bumps and holes in the road surface. Shock absorbers are mounted over the **wheels**.
The car's shock absorbers gave them a comfortable ride, even over a bumpy road.

short-takeoff-and-landing aircraft *noun*

A short-takeoff-and-landing aircraft is an **airplane** that is designed to use a short runway. It has very large, movable flaps at the back, and slats on the front of the wings. These allow it to rise or fall steeply and quickly. The abbreviation for short-takeoff-and-landing aircraft is STOL.
The short-takeoff-and-landing aircraft was able to land safely at a clearing in the jungle.

shortwave radio *noun*

Shortwave radio is a method of **transmitting** and **receiving** signals by **radio**. A shortwave radio **transmitter** can send signals all around the world. These signals are bounced back, or reflected, by a part of Earth's atmosphere called the ionosphere.
He listened to a concert broadcast from Australia by shortwave radio.

shutter *noun*

A shutter is the part of a **camera** between the **lens** and the **film**. When a button or **lever** is pressed, the shutter opens and light passes through the lens of the camera and exposes the film. Many cameras have adjustable shutter speeds that can range from one two-thousandth of a second to 30 seconds. Some cameras have **electronic** shutters that automatically adjust speeds.
The shutter can be set to open for different lengths of time for different amounts of light.

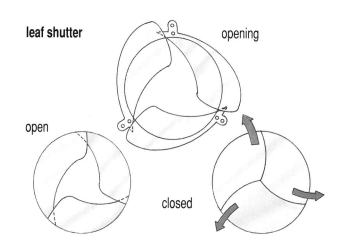

leaf shutter   opening

open

closed

sensors and detectors *nouns*

Sensors and detectors are **devices** that react to certain events called stimuli. Sensors in a **robot** allow it to find the correct position for it to do work. A smoke detector gives a warning if fire breaks out.
Burglar alarm systems contain sensors and detectors.

One type of burglar alarm gives out, or emits, rays called microwaves. The microwaves detect movement anywhere in the room and trigger an alarm bell.

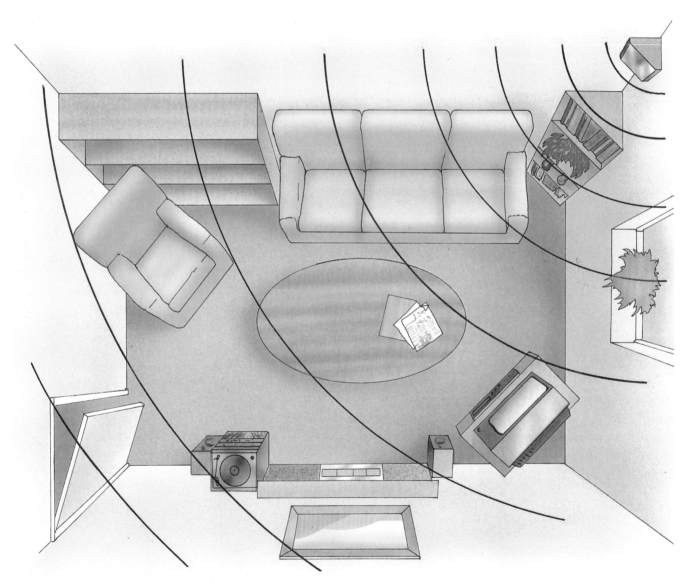

Another type of burglar alarm emits ultrasonic rays. They detect the slightest sound made by a person entering the room.

A third type of burglar alarm emits infrared rays. These detect the body heat given off by someone entering the room.

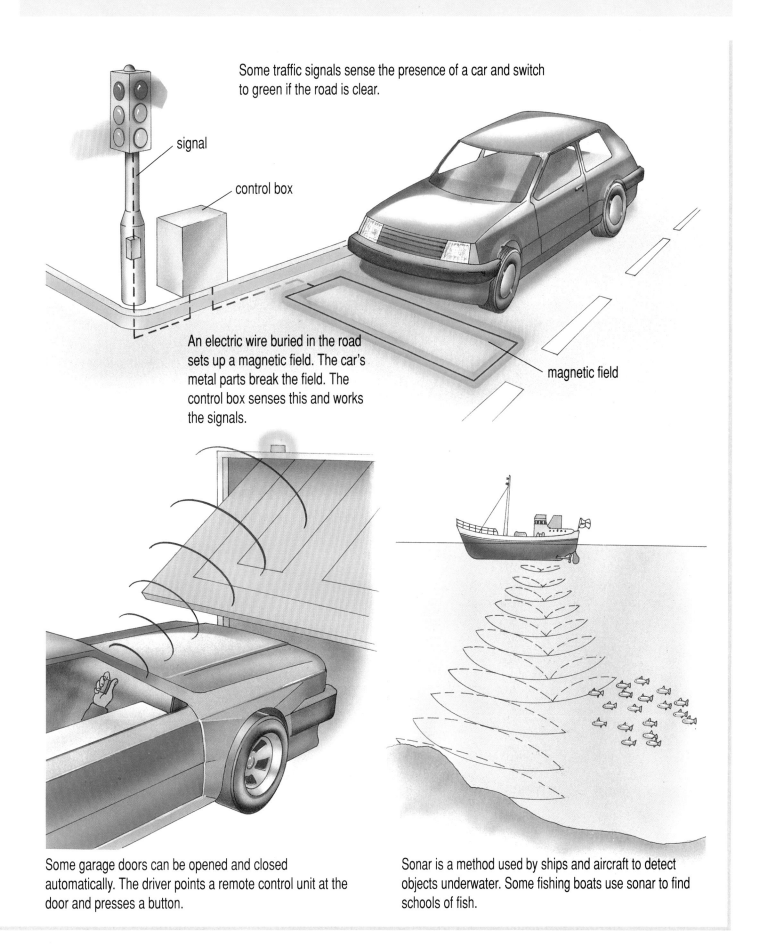

Some traffic signals sense the presence of a car and switch to green if the road is clear.

signal

control box

An electric wire buried in the road sets up a magnetic field. The car's metal parts break the field. The control box senses this and works the signals.

magnetic field

Some garage doors can be opened and closed automatically. The driver points a remote control unit at the door and presses a button.

Sonar is a method used by ships and aircraft to detect objects underwater. Some fishing boats use sonar to find schools of fish.

ship   *noun*

A ship is a large **boat** that goes to sea. There are many different kinds of ships. For hundreds of years, all ships had sails and were powered by the wind. Today they usually have **steam turbines** or **diesel engines**. Some ships are **nuclear powered**. *A cargo ship carries raw materials and goods from one port to another.*

This Spanish galleon was used in the early 1600s as a trading and fighting ship.

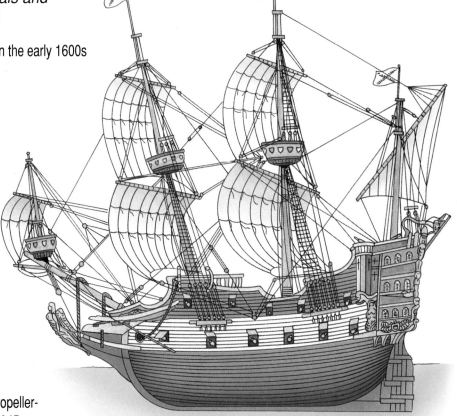

The SS *Great Britain* was the first propeller-driven ship to cross the Atlantic, in 1845.

This picture of the *Queen Elizabeth II* passenger liner has been cut away to show the main areas.

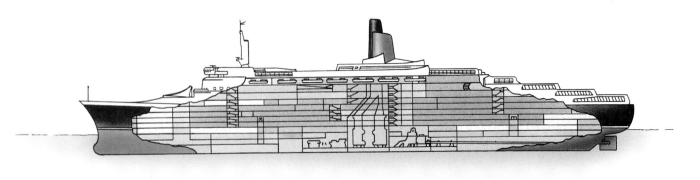

☐ other	☐ crew's quarters
☐ passenger cabins and lounges	☐ restaurants and kitchen
☐ cargo and supplies	☐ recreation areas
☐ fuel and engine room	

The *Savannah* was an American nuclear-powered merchant ship launched in 1959.

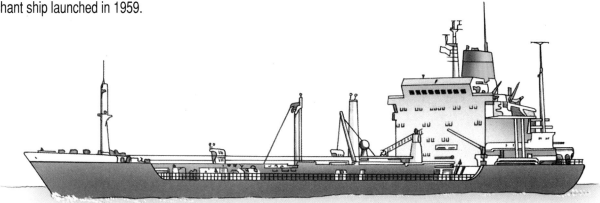

This oil tanker was built to carry petroleum from oil terminals.

shuttle   *noun*

A shuttle is a part of a **loom**. It carries one of the threads which are being woven and passes it over and under the other, vertical threads.

Several different shuttles are used in a loom which is weaving cloth with a colored pattern.

signal   *noun*

1. A signal is a message. **Electric signals** can be sent along wires or through the air using **radio**. Telephone calls and radio and television programmes are made up of signals.

We could not get a clear picture on the television because lightning disturbed the signal.

2. A signal is a **device** used to show whether a road or railway is safe to be used. Most signals use lights colored red for danger, green for safe and amber or yellow for caution.

The train driver stopped because the signal showed red.

silencer   *noun*

A silencer is a **device** that makes **engines** run quietly. It passes **exhaust gases** through a series of perforated pipes lined with a special material. The material takes in, or absorbs, sound. All **vehicles**, such as cars and motorcycles, are fitted with a silencer.

The car made a loud noise because it had a hole in its silencer.

silicon chip   *noun*

A silicon chip is a kind of crystal that is made from a tiny piece of a material called silicon. A silicon chip has **electric circuits** cut, or etched, on it. It is surrounded by a plastic case to protect it from damage. There are many silicon chips in a **computer**.

Some silicon chips are only one twelfth of an inch square.

simulator ► flight simulator

simple machines ► page 124

single lens reflex camera   *noun*

A single lens reflex, or SLR, camera is a **camera** that has a special viewfinder. When you look through the viewfinder, you see exactly what will be in the photograph you are going to take. Prisms and a mirror bend, or reflect, the light waves onto the viewfinder lens.

You cannot see through the viewfinder of a single lens reflex camera while the picture is being taken.

siphon   *noun*

A siphon is a **device** for transferring liquids from one container to another. It is a curved tube or pipe. One end of the siphon must be placed in the liquid to be transferred and the other end in a container placed on a lower level than the liquid. If the siphon is full of liquid to start with, it will allow the higher container to empty into the lower.

He used a siphon to empty the gasoline out of the car's gasoline tank.

siren   *noun*

A siren is a kind of whistle that makes a loud, wailing sound. Police, fire, and ambulance vehicles are equipped with sirens to warn of their approach. Sirens are also used in times of war to alert people to air raids.

The ambulance driver switched on his siren before driving through the heavy traffic.

skate   *noun*

A skate is a frame with a blade or wheels fixed to a shoe. Ice skates have metal blades that allow a person to glide over ice. Ice skating is an Olympic sport. Roller skates have small wheels and can be used on any smooth, hard surface. The wheels contain ball bearings that help to keep the moving parts turning smoothly. People wearing skates can travel very fast.

She put on her ice skates and glided over the frozen lake.

sled *noun*
A sled is a wooden frame that is designed to move downhill across snow or ice. Boards are mounted on runners that slide smoothly over the surface causing little **friction**. The passenger rides on the boards.
She guided the sled down the slope using her body weight and her arms to steer it.

slide projector *noun*
A slide projector is an **appliance** that shows still pictures on a screen. The pictures are projected from special **photographs** called transparencies. These allow a bright light to shine through to a **lens**, which throws the picture onto the screen.
They used their slide projector to show us some photographs of their vacation.

SLR camera ▶ **single lens reflex camera**

smelting *noun*
Smelting is the process of obtaining metals from metal ores. The ore is heated in a **furnace** and the metal is separated from the waste, or **slag**.
Smelting is done in a foundry.

smoke detector ▶ **sensors and detectors**

snow blower *noun*
A snow blower is a **vehicle** that clears snow. It has a **fan** that sends out a stream of air and blows the snow to the side.
The airport was closed until a snow blower had cleared the runways.

socket *noun*
1. A socket is a **device** with holes in it to fit the **terminals** on an electric plug.
An appliance is connected to the electricity supply by pushing a plug into a socket.
2. A socket is a part of some **machines**. It is a hollow into which another part fits and is held in place, but is free to move.
The gear lever fit into the gearbox socket.

software *noun*
Software is the **data** and **programs** that a **computer** uses. It is loaded into the computer's **hardware** and may be stored on **floppy disks** or **magnetic tape**.
Software gives a computer instructions and the information that allows it to do its work.

solar heater *noun*
A solar heater is a **device** that heats water by using energy from the Sun. The energy is collected by **solar panels** mounted on the roof of a building. The solar panels contain black plates and water pipes, and a **pump** sends the heated water to a **boiler** and **radiators**.
The solar heater kept the house warm in winter.

solar panel *noun*
A solar panel is a **device** for collecting energy from the Sun for use in a **solar heater** or to **generate electricity**. Solar panels have black plates because black absorbs heat from sunlight better than other colors.
Solar panels are mounted on the roofs of buildings or on the ground facing the Sun.

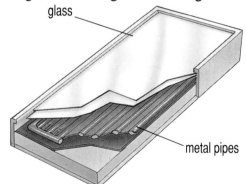
glass
metal pipes

solenoid *noun*
A solenoid is a part of an **electromagnet**. It is a **coil** of wire wound around an **iron** bar. When **electric current** flows through a solenoid, it creates a magnetic **force**, which can be used to operate other **devices**. Solenoids are found in **relays** and electric doors.
A solenoid was used to operate the railroad crossing gates

simple machines   *noun*

A simple machine is a **device** that does work. It lessens the amount of effort needed for work to be done. As with all machines, a simple machine needs a source of energy for it to work.

The six simple machines are a screw, a wedge, an inclined plane, a pulley, a lever and a wheel and axle.

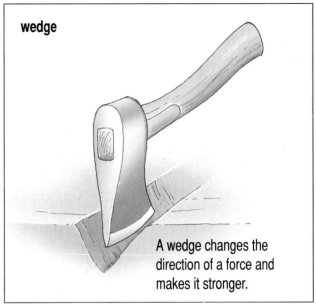

wedge

A wedge changes the direction of a force and makes it stronger.

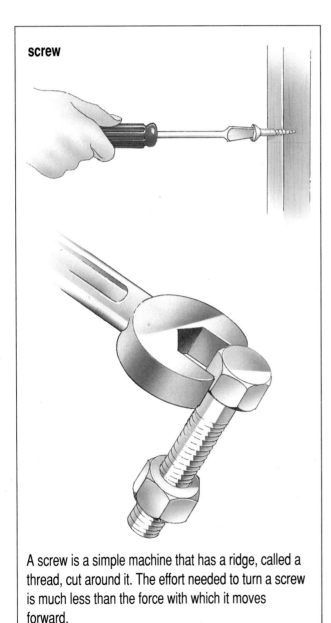

screw

A screw is a simple machine that has a ridge, called a thread, cut around it. The effort needed to turn a screw is much less than the force with which it moves forward.

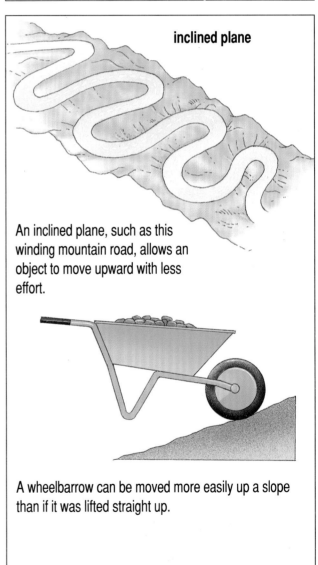

inclined plane

An inclined plane, such as this winding mountain road, allows an object to move upward with less effort.

A wheelbarrow can be moved more easily up a slope than if it was lifted straight up.

pulley

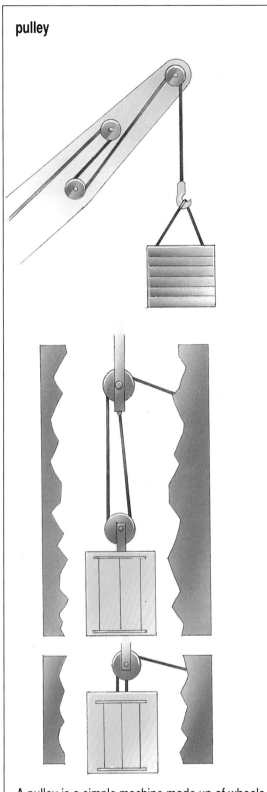

A pulley is a simple machine made up of wheels and ropes. It changes the direction of the pull, or lifting force. It is easier to pull down on something than to lift it up.

lever

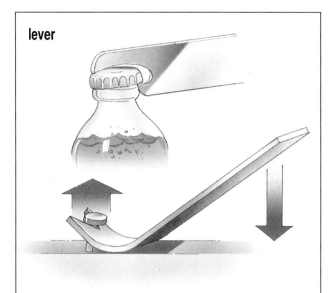

A lever is a bar or rod that moves around a fulcrum. The effort of pressing down on one end lifts a load.

wheel and axle

A wheel and axle is part of many machines. It can pass, or transmit, a turning motion from one part of a machine to another.

solid-fuel rocket   *noun*
A solid-fuel rocket is a **rocket engine** that
burns fuel that is solid. A fireworks rocket is
an example of a solid-fuel rocket. Its fuel is a
kind of gunpowder.
The sailors sent up an alarm by using a
solid-fuel rocket called a flare.

sonar   *noun*
Sonar is a **device** on some **ships** that works
in a way similar to **radar**. Sonar is used to
find objects underwater. It gives out very
high-pitched sound waves, which are
bounced back, or reflected, by the objects,
marking their location.
The fishermen used sonar to find schools of
fish.

sonic boom   *noun*
A sonic boom is the very loud sound made
by an airplane moving faster than the speed
of sound. The airplane produces a cone-
shaped shockwave, and when this reaches
the ground, we hear it as a "boom."
The jet produced a sonic boom.

space probe   *noun*
A space probe is a **spacecraft** that does not
carry a crew. Instead they carry **cameras**
and many other instruments to study the
planets they visit. A space probe sends
information back to Earth by **radio waves**.
The space probe was sent into orbit the
planet Venus.

space shuttle   *noun*
A space shuttle is a kind of reusable
spacecraft that travels between Earth and
space. A space shuttle can carry astronauts
and equipment to a **space station** in orbit. It
can also launch **satellites**. At the end of the
mission the space shuttle lands like an
airplane.
The space shuttle carried a new crew out to
the space station.

space station   *noun*
A space station is a manned **satellite** that
stays in space for a long time. Space
stations are used to carry out research.
Their crews of astronauts can be exchanged
by means of a **space shuttle**.
Scientists hope to build a space station that
can hold up to 30 people.

spacecraft   *noun*
A spacecraft is a **vehicle** that is sent into
space. It may have a crew or it may be
unmanned. Some spacecraft are sent into
orbit around Earth or another of the planets.
Others make short journeys and return to
Earth.
There was a roar from the rocket engine and
the spacecraft lifted off.

spade   *noun*
A spade is a tool used for digging.
It usually consists of a wooden shaft with a
handle attached to a rectangular blade
made of iron or steel. A spade is a kind of
shovel.
The spade was used to dig up rows of
potatoes.

spark plug   *noun*
A spark plug is a part of some **internal**
combustion engines. One spark plug fits
into each of the **cylinders**. When it receives
an **electric current**, it makes a spark that
ignites the mixture of **fuel** and air in the
cylinder.
The car engine was not firing properly
because its spark plugs were dirty.

spectacles *plural noun*
Spectacles are **devices** that help people with poor sight to see more clearly. They are two **lenses** held in place in a frame. They refocus the image on the lens of the eye.
Spectacles are also known as eyeglasses.

speedometer *noun*
A speedometer is the part of a **vehicle** that shows how fast the vehicle is traveling. A land vehicle speedometer is connected by a **cable** and **gears** to the **transmission**. It shows the speed of a vehicle by means of a pointer and **dial**.
The speedometer showed that the car was traveling far too fast.

spindle *noun*
1. A spindle is a metal rod on which part of a **machine** turns round, or **rotates**.
An axle is a kind of spindle.
2. A spindle is part of a **spinning machine**. It is a metal pin used for twisting and winding the thread.
The spindles on the spinning machine were full of thread and ready to be used for weaving the material.

spin dryer *noun*
A spin dryer is an **appliance** used in the home. It dries wet laundry by spinning it fast inside a drum. The water is thrown out of the drum by **centrifugal force**. A heater finishes the drying process. A spin dryer is useful if clothes need to be dried quickly.
A spin dryer is also sometimes called an automatic clothes dryer.

spinning machine *noun*
A spinning machine is a machine for making yarn or thread out of **raw material**. It straightens out the fibers of the raw material and then twists them together evenly, forming a long string or yarn.
At the factory there was a spinning machine making woolen yarn from sheep's wool.

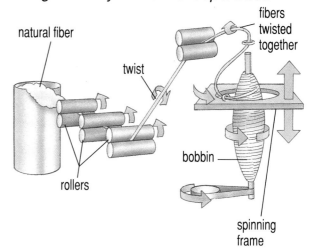

spirit level *noun*
A spirit level is a **tool** used to make sure that a surface is level. A spirit level contains a **glass** or **plastic** tube, inside of which is a liquid with a bubble of air in it. The spirit level is placed on the surface to be checked. If the bubble is exactly in the center of the tube, the surface is level.
The carpenter used a spirit level to check that the floor did not slope.

spring *noun*
A spring is a part of many **machines**. It may be a **coil** or a bar made of a special type of **steel**. Springs return to their original form if they are pushed out of shape. The **axles** of **vehicles** have springs fitted to them to make them travel more smoothly. If the **wheel** of a car goes over a bump, the springs that are positioned between the body of the car and the wheels absorb the shock. This stops the passengers from feeling a sharp bump.
His bicycle seat was uncomfortable because one of the springs had broken.
spring *verb*

127

spring balance *noun*
A spring balance is a kind of **weighing machine**. It contains a **coil spring**, which is fixed at the top. The object to be weighed is hung on a hook at the lower end of the spring. A needle is pulled down along a **scale** and shows the weight of the object.
He used a spring balance to find the weight of the fruit.

sprinkler ► **lawn sprinkler**

sprinkler system *noun*
A sprinkler system is a method of putting out a fire. It is found in many buildings, such as large stores. The system contains fire **detectors**. If any of these detects a fire, the sprinklers are turned on automatically. They spread a fine spray of water over the area and put out the fire.
The fire in the factory did little damage because the sprinkler system put it out.

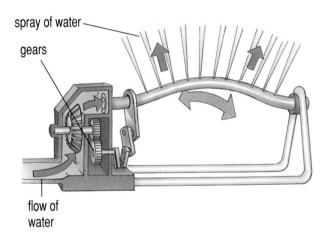

spray of water

gears

flow of water

sprocket *noun*
Sprockets are pointed teeth on the outside edge of a **wheel** that fit into, or mesh with, the links of a chain. When the wheel turns, its sprockets move the chain and the chain moves another wheel, which also has sprokets. The distance between the sprockets' teeth must be the same as the distance between the chain links. This distance is called the pitch of the sprocket.
Sprockets on the pedal wheel of a bicycle grip the chain and make the rear wheel turn.

spur gears *plural noun*
Spur gears are parts of some **machines**. They are used when a **drive shaft** makes another **shaft** turn at the same angle.
The teeth of spur gears are cut so that they are parallel with the shaft.

spy satellite *noun*
A spy satellite is a **satellite** in orbit around Earth. It is used by one country to find out what is happening in another. **Television cameras** on the spy satellite take pictures, which are sent back to Earth.
The spy satellite showed that there was a large army in the desert.

stabilizer *noun*
A stabilizer is a **device** fitted to many **ships**. It helps to keep a ship from rolling in heavy seas. Stabilizers are shaped like fins and are fitted in pairs, one on each side of the ship, below the water line. Each fin can be tilted automatically to prevent the ship from being affected by the action of the waves.
They had a pleasant voyage because the ship was equipped with stabilizers.

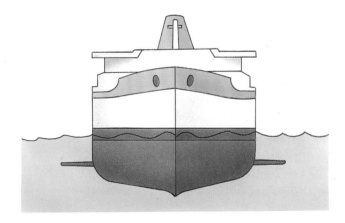

stapler *noun*
A stapler is a **device** for fastening things together. A staple is a short length of wire. The stapler pushes the staple into the materials being fastened. When a stapler is used for paper, it bends the ends of the staple over once it is in place, holding the papers securely.
She bound the pages with a staple.

starter motor   *noun*
A starter motor is the part of a **vehicle** that provides a surge of **power** through a **gearwheel** to turn the **crankshaft** and start the **engine**. A starter motor is driven by **electricity** which flows from the vehicle's **battery**.
My car would not start because there was not enough energy in the battery to turn the starter motor.

static electricity   *noun*
Static electricity is a kind of natural energy that builds up when **electrons** move from one object to another. It does not flow steadily like an **electric current** but stays still or leaps between objects.
Lightning is caused by static electricity leaping between clouds or between a cloud and the ground.

stator   *noun*
A stator is a part of a **machine**. It is an **electromagnet** inside an **electric motor** or a **generator**. A stator stays still while **coils** of wire spin around it.
The movement of the coils around the stator generates electricity.

steam engine   *noun*
A steam engine is a kind of **engine** that produces energy from boiling water. The pressure of steam from the boiling water is used to drive a **piston**, which in turn can drive **wheels** or operate **machinery**.
We had a ride on a railroad train pulled by a steam engine.

steam locomotive ► **steam engine**

steam roller   *noun*
A steam roller is a **machine** that used to make or repair roads. At the front, in place of **wheels**, it has a heavy **roller** that presses on the road surface and makes it hard. The rear wheels are also heavy rollers.
The construction workers used a steam roller to give the road a new surface.

steam turbine   *noun*
A steam turbine is a kind of **steam engine**. Steam is made by boiling water and forcing it at high pressure through a set of **turbine wheels**. These have slits between them, and the **force** of the steam makes the turbine wheels turn and drive a **shaft**.
Some ships are powered by steam turbines.

steel   *noun*
Steel is a metal made by mixing **iron** with other substances. It is made in a **furnace**. Many different kinds of steel are used in **machines**.
Stainless steel is a kind of steel that does not rust.

steel convertor   *noun*
A steel convertor is a piece of equipment for making **steel**. It melts **iron** in a **vessel** and **pumps** air through the molten metal. This forces impure substances to float to the surface. When the steel is pure enough, the vessel is tipped and the steel is poured into molds.
Many different kinds of steel can be made in a steel convertor.

steering   *noun*
Steering is a means of changing the direction of a **vehicle**, **ship**, or **aircraft**. A road vehicle is steered by turning a steering **wheel** connected by **gears** to the front wheels. Ships and aircraft are steered by a **rudder**. **Bicycles** and **motorcycles** are steered by turning the handlebars.
The racing car had excellent steering.
steer   *verb*

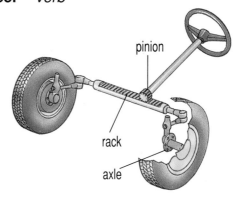
pinion
rack
axle

submarine   *noun*

A submarine is a kind of **boat** that can travel under the surface of the water. A submarine contains tanks that are filled with water to make it sink. Most submarines are **warships** and can fire **torpedoes** or **nuclear weapons**. Some submarines can travel underwater for many months.

They watched as the submarine filled its tanks with water and dived.

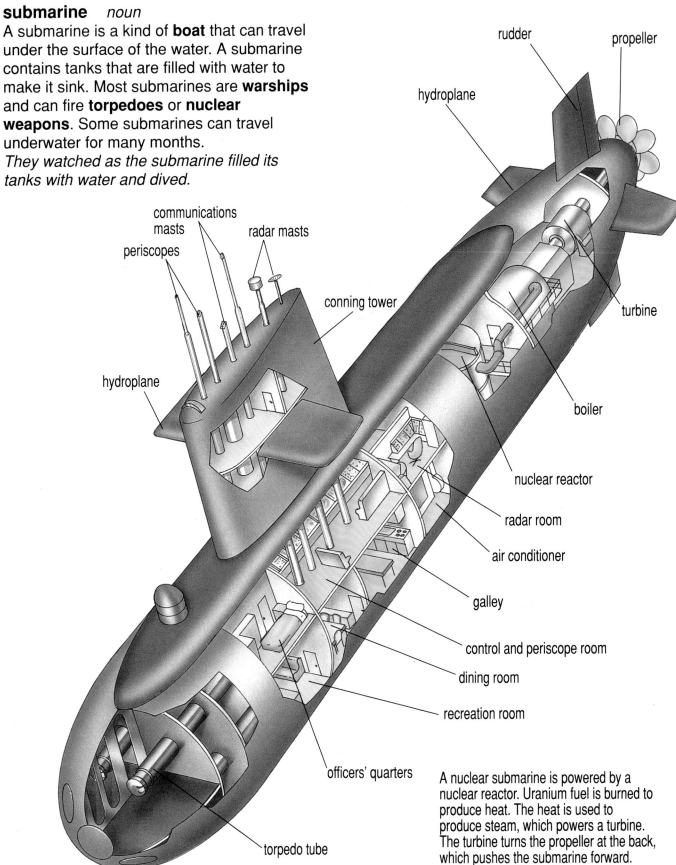

communications masts
radar masts
periscopes
rudder
propeller
hydroplane
turbine
conning tower
boiler
hydroplane
nuclear reactor
radar room
air conditioner
galley
control and periscope room
dining room
recreation room
officers' quarters
torpedo tube

A nuclear submarine is powered by a nuclear reactor. Uranium fuel is burned to produce heat. The heat is used to produce steam, which powers a turbine. The turbine turns the propeller at the back, which pushes the submarine forward.

A submersible is a small submarine.
It is used by scientists to explore the
deep parts of the ocean. It can also be
used to take divers down to the seabed
to repair underwater pipelines.

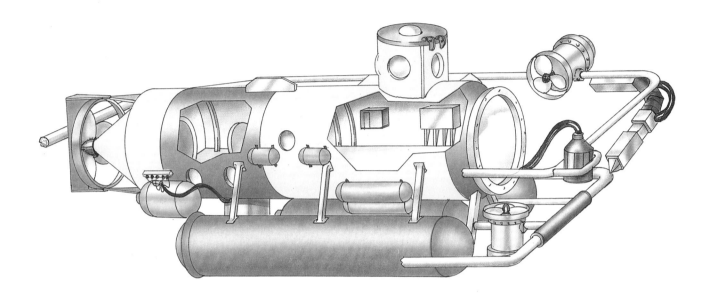

How a submarine dives and surfaces

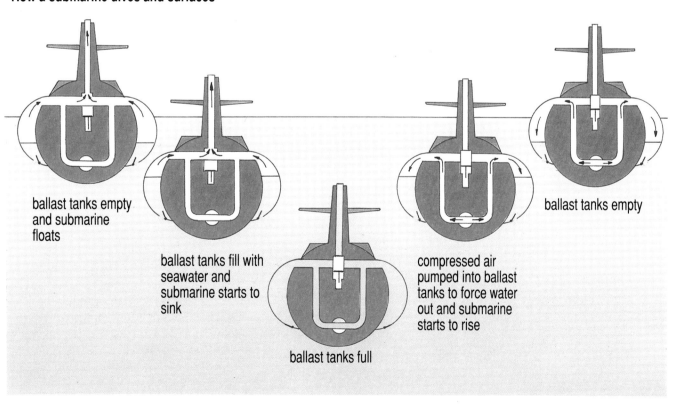

ballast tanks empty
and submarine
floats

ballast tanks fill with
seawater and
submarine starts to
sink

ballast tanks full

compressed air
pumped into ballast
tanks to force water
out and submarine
starts to rise

ballast tanks empty

stereo- *prefix*
Stereo- describes things that are made to seem real or solid. The various sounds from a stereophonic **tape** or **compact disk** come from different loudspeakers which make the sound richer. A **stereoscope** makes a picture seem three-dimensional.
Human beings have two eyes, which give them stereoscopic vision.

stethoscope *noun*
A stethoscope is an instrument used by doctors to hear the beating of the heart and the sound of air in the lungs. A stethoscope is a tube with an earpiece at one end. At the other end, a **device** with a **sensor** is placed against the body.
The doctor listened to her lungs with a stethoscope.

STOL *noun*
STOL means short takeoff and landing. It is a type of aircraft that needs a much shorter distance to take off and land than conventional aircraft. It is usually slower than a normal airplane.
The STOL landed on the short runway of the old airfield.

stopwatch *noun*
A stopwatch is a special kind of **watch** that can be started or stopped at any time. It is used to time races and other sports events. Some stopwatches have a **clockwork motor**. Others have **electronic** parts.
Some stopwatches are so accurate that they can measure hundredths of a second.

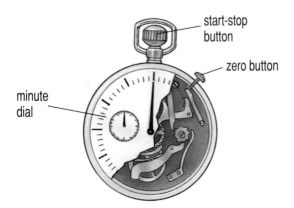

minute dial

start-stop button

zero button

streamlined *adjective*
Streamlined describes the shape of some objects. Streamlined surfaces are curved, so that air or water can flow over them easily. *Submarines, airplanes, and most cars have streamlined shapes.*

structure *noun*
A structure is an object that has been built. Bridges, buildings, tunnels, towers, and **oil rigs** are some kinds of structures. Some structures, like houses shelter people. Other structures support things. For example, a pillar might support a state. Structures can also span things, like a bridge that connects one side of a river to the other.
The structure being built is a new office building.

submarine ▶ page 130

submersible *noun*
A submersible is a very small kind of **submarine**. It is used to carry out underwater repairs to **oil rigs** and other **structures**. Submersibles are often fitted with **robots** and other **tools** that can be operated from inside.
Two men in a submersible went down to examine the damage to the oil rig.

subway *noun*
A subway is an underground electric railway used as public transportation. New York; Washington, D.C. and Boston are among the American cities with subways.
London has a subway called the Underground, and Paris has one called the Metro.

sun gear ▶ planetary gears

superheated *adjective*
Superheated describes a liquid or **gas** that is heated to a very high pressure. The liquid or gas can then be used to drive an **engine** or a **turbine**.
Steam locomotives are powered by superheated steam.

supermarket checkout   *noun*
A supermarket checkout is the place in a supermarket where you pay for what you have selected. It has an **electronic** cash register that adds up the amount you have to pay. The checkout may also have equipment that reads **bar codes** to look up the prices and keep track of the goods in stock.
The cash register at the supermarket checkout produced a list of what he had bought.

supersonic   *adjective*
Supersonic describes a speed faster than the speed of sound. This is about 760 miles per hour, depending on how dense and humid the air is.
The Concorde is a supersonic airliner.

swing-wing aircraft   *noun*
Swing-wing aircraft are **airplanes** whose wings can swing backward or forward during flight. The wings swing forward for takeoff or landing. In level flight, they swing backward so they become **streamlined** and air flows more easily over them.
Many fighters are swing-wing aircraft.

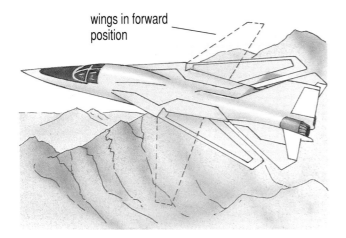

wings in forward position

synthesizer   *noun*
A synthesizer is a musical instrument that uses **electronics** and **computers** to produce many different kinds of sound. A synthesizer is played by using a **keyboard**.
The rock group included two electric guitars and a synthesizer.

synthetic   *adjective*
Synthetic describes things that are made by people and are not natural. Cotton is a natural fiber, but **nylon** is a synthetic one. **Plastics** are synthetic materials.
Her new dress was made from a mixture of natural and synthetic fibers.

syringe   *noun*
A syringe is a kind of **pump**. It is a **cylinder** containing a **piston**. There is a nozzle at one end and a small handle at the other. Liquid is drawn into the cylinder through the nozzle and then pushed out again. Doctors often use syringes to inject medicines.
The doctor used a syringe to give me an injection to prevent hay fever.

tanker *noun*
1. A tanker is a kind of **ship** that carries large amounts of a liquid cargo. Some tankers carry **petroleum** or petroleum **products**.
They went to watch the oil tanker docking at the oil terminal.
2. A tanker is a road **vehicle** that carries a **load** such as **oil**, flour, or sugar. The load is carried in a large tank behind the driver's cab.
The tanker delivered a fresh supply of gasoline to the filling station.

tap *noun*
A tap is a **device** for controlling the flow of liquids. It is a kind of **valve**. When a tap is turned on, it allows the liquid to flow out. The flow of liquid is stopped when the tap is turned off.
She turned on the hot and cold water taps to fill the bath.

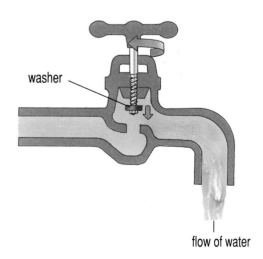

washer

flow of water

tape ► **magnetic tape**

tape head *noun*
A tape head is a part of a **tape recorder**. When the tape recorder is recording or playing, **magnetic tape** is pressed against the tape head. **Electric signals** pass from the tape through the head to the **amplifier**.
You can buy a special tape to clean the tape heads of a tape recorder.

tape recorder ► page 135

telecommunication *noun*
Telecommunication is the way people communicate with each other using **electric signals**. It started with the invention of the **telegraph**, which marked the beginning of the telecommunications age as we know it today. Telecommunications can travel by **radio waves**, along wires, or along **fiber optic cables**.
Radio, television, the telephone, and fax machine are different kinds of telecommunications.

telegraph *noun*
A telegraph is a **device** for sending messages over long distances. The messages are sent along a wire in a **code**, which is made up of long and short bursts of **electricity** that stand for letters of the alphabet. The operator taps out these bursts with a **key** or finger pad. Telegraph messages are received by a **loudspeaker** or on a paper tape.
The soldiers sent back a report from the battlefield by telegraph.

telephone *noun*
A telephone is an instrument for communicating over a distance. When someone speaks into the **mouthpiece** of a telephone, the sounds are changed into **electric signals**. These travel along a wire or **fiber optic cable** to the person at the other end. Then the signals are changed back into sound.
She had some important news to tell her friend, so she used the telephone.

tape recorder   *noun*

A tape recorder is a **machine** that records **electric signals** on **magnetic tape**. The signals can be sounds, pictures, or **computer programs**. A tape recorder can also play back the signals to a **loudspeaker**, **television** set, or computer.

He listened to the sound of his own voice on his tape recorder.

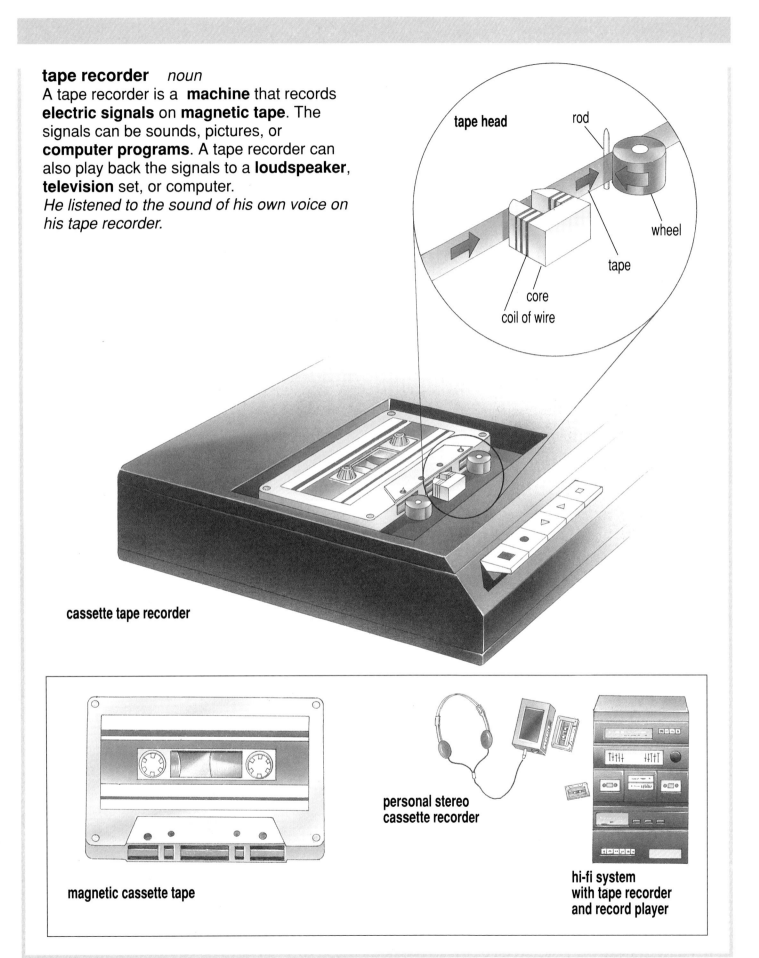

tape head

rod

wheel

tape

core

coil of wire

cassette tape recorder

magnetic cassette tape

personal stereo cassette recorder

hi-fi system with tape recorder and record player

135

telephoto lens   *noun*
A telephoto lens is a **device** that can be fitted to a **camera** to take a close-up **photograph** of a distant object. It is made up of a number of **lenses**. It works like a **telescope** and makes objects seem larger and nearer.
He used a telephoto lens to take a photograph of the distant shore.

telescope ► page 138

teletext   *noun*
Teletext is printed information that appears on home **television screens**. It is sent from the **transmitter**, together with ordinary television pictures, but it is hidden from view above and below the screen. A **device** called a decoder is needed to bring teletext information into view on the screen.
The teletext showed us a list of what was playing at all the theaters in the city.

teletypewriter   *noun*
A teletypewriter is a **machine** for sending and **receiving** printed messages. A message is put into a teletypewriter using a **keyboard**. The teletypewriter changes the message into **electric signals** and sends them along wires or by **radio**. Another teletypewriter changes the signals back into letters and numbers and prints them on paper.
Newspaper reporters often use teletypewriters to send reports back to their newspapers.

television ► page 140

television camera   *noun*
A television camera is a special **camera** used to take **television** pictures. It contains **electron guns** that **scan** the scene in front of the camera and turn light and colors into **electric signals**. These signals are sent down a wire to a **transmitter**.
In most television shows, several television cameras are used to capture the action.

television satellite   *noun*
A television satellite is a **satellite** that **receives television** signals from a **transmitter** and sends them back to Earth. It remains over the same part of Earth's surface.
Television satellites are used to broadcast events that are happening on the other side of the world.

television set   *noun*
A television set is an **appliance** that **receives** and shows **television** programs. It collects **electric signals** from an **aerial** or **cable** and changes them into pictures and sound. The electric signals cause an **electron gun** to fire **electrons** at the television **screen**. Pictures are produced on a screen and the sounds are heard on a **loudspeaker**.
Most families own a television set.

telex   *noun*
Telex is a form of **telecommunication** that links **teletypewriters** together by **telephone** lines as a way of sending written messages.
He sent a telex message to say when he would be arriving in New York.

temperature gauge   *noun*
A temperature gauge is a **device** that shows the temperature of a liquid, solid, or **gas**. It shows the temperature on a **dial**. Many **machines** are equipped with temperature gauges to make sure that they do not overheat or become too cold.
The temperature gauge showed that the water in the car engine was nearly boiling.

tension   *noun*
Tension is a kind of **force** that tries to stretch an object. There is tension in a string that is being pulled down by a weight. The opposite of tension is compression.
Tension in the spokes makes a bicycle wheel retain its round shape.

terminal   *noun*
1. A terminal is a special dock where **petroleum** or petroleum **products** are unloaded and stored.
The oil tanker docked at the terminal, and unloaded its cargo.
2. A terminal is part of an **electric circuit**. It connects a **device** to the **electricity** supply. A **battery** has a negative and positive terminal. **Bulb** holders and most switches have two terminals.
He screwed the electric wires into the terminals.

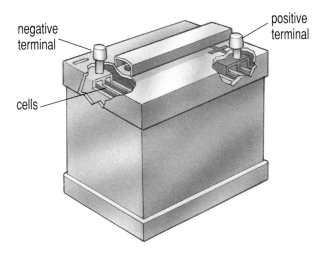

negative terminal

positive terminal

cells

thermometer   *noun*
A thermometer is an instrument that measures temperature. Most thermometers have a liquid inside a thin, **glass** tube. When the liquid is warmed, it expands and rises up the tube. The temperature shows on a **scale**.
The doctor slipped a thermometer under her tongue and took her temperature.

thermonuclear weapon ► **nuclear weapon**

thermostat   *noun*
A thermostat is a **device** that controls a **boiler** or a **heater**. It can be set to switch the boiler or heater off when a certain temperature is reached. Then it switches it on again when the temperature falls. A thermostat contains a thin strip of metal. When the strip heats up, it bends and works a switch.
If the temperature falls, a thermostat automatically switches on the heater.

throttle   *noun*
A throttle is the valve that controls the amount of **fuel** and air flowing into an **engine**. Opening the throttle makes the engine give out more **power**.
The gas pedal of a car is connected to the throttle.

thruster ► **afterburner**

ticket machine   *noun*
A ticket machine is a **machine** that automatically issues tickets when money is placed in it. Ticket machines are found at some train stations and parking lots.
He bought a ticket for the trip from a ticket machine.

tidal power   *noun*
Tidal power is energy produced by the rise and fall of the sea's tides. The flow of water can be used to drive a **turbine** and make **electricity**.
There is a tidal power station at Rance, in France.

telescope *noun*

A telescope is an **optical instrument** used to study the night sky. It contains **lenses** and **mirrors** that make distant objects look closer.

You can see the 'mountains of the Moon' clearly if you look at the Moon through a telescope.

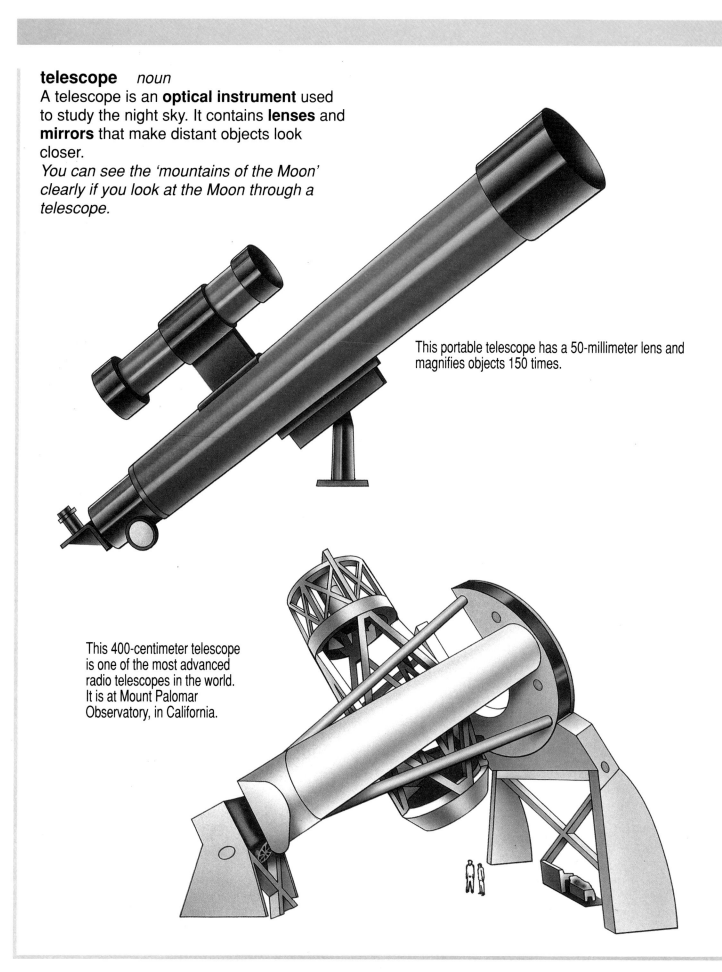

This portable telescope has a 50-millimeter lens and magnifies objects 150 times.

This 400-centimeter telescope is one of the most advanced radio telescopes in the world. It is at Mount Palomar Observatory, in California.

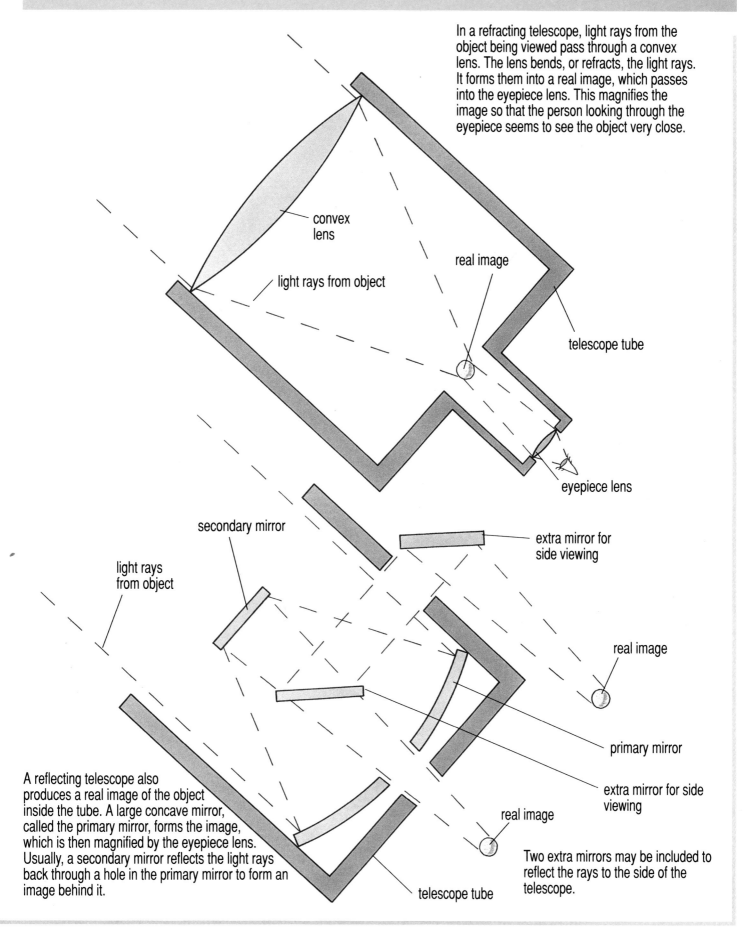

In a refracting telescope, light rays from the object being viewed pass through a convex lens. The lens bends, or refracts, the light rays. It forms them into a real image, which passes into the eyepiece lens. This magnifies the image so that the person looking through the eyepiece seems to see the object very close.

convex lens

light rays from object

real image

telescope tube

eyepiece lens

secondary mirror

extra mirror for side viewing

light rays from object

real image

primary mirror

extra mirror for side viewing

A reflecting telescope also produces a real image of the object inside the tube. A large concave mirror, called the primary mirror, forms the image, which is then magnified by the eyepiece lens. Usually, a secondary mirror reflects the light rays back through a hole in the primary mirror to form an image behind it.

real image

Two extra mirrors may be included to reflect the rays to the side of the telescope.

telescope tube

television *noun*

Television is a method of sending and **receiving** sounds and pictures over a distance. It uses **radio waves** to carry **electric signals**.

Television is the main source of entertainment for many people.

Electronic circuits change electric signals into sound, which comes out through a loudspeaker.

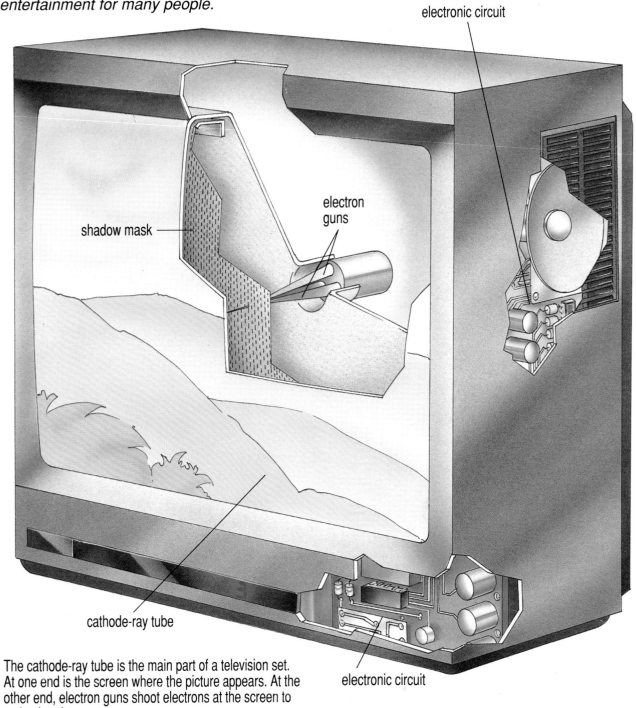

electronic circuit

electron guns

shadow mask

cathode-ray tube

electronic circuit

The cathode-ray tube is the main part of a television set. At one end is the screen where the picture appears. At the other end, electron guns shoot electrons at the screen to make the picture.

There is a metal shadow mask behind the television screen, with rows of holes punched in it. The screen is coated with tiny dots of phosphorus, arranged in groups of three. The dots glow green, blue and red when electrons are fired at them. Three electron guns fire electrons through the holes in the shadow mask, so that each gun lights up the right color.

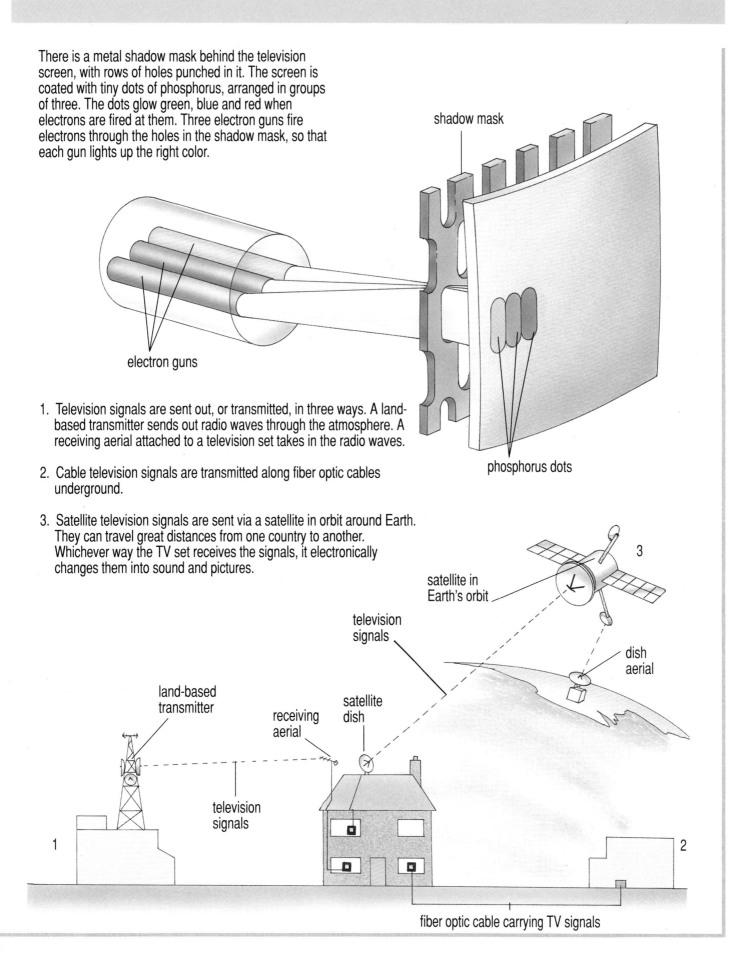

electron guns

shadow mask

phosphorus dots

1. Television signals are sent out, or transmitted, in three ways. A land-based transmitter sends out radio waves through the atmosphere. A receiving aerial attached to a television set takes in the radio waves.

2. Cable television signals are transmitted along fiber optic cables underground.

3. Satellite television signals are sent via a satellite in orbit around Earth. They can travel great distances from one country to another. Whichever way the TV set receives the signals, it electronically changes them into sound and pictures.

satellite in Earth's orbit

television signals

dish aerial

land-based transmitter

receiving aerial

satellite dish

television signals

1

2

3

fiber optic cable carrying TV signals

till *noun*
A till, or cash register, is a machine which is found in shops. Some tills work out how much a customer has to pay and how much change is to be given. Tills provide printed receipts from a roll of paper.
The shop assistant put the money in the till and gave me the change and a receipt.

tire *noun*
A tire is the rubber covering on the outside edge of a **wheel**. It can be made of solid rubber or it can be a **pneumatic tire**. A tire has a pattern called the tread on its surface. This helps it to grip the road. Tires are used on airplanes, road vehicles and many other kinds of machines.
I went to the bicycle shop and bought two new tires for my bicycle.

titanium *noun*
Titanium is a metal. It is very hard and stands up to high temperatures. It is added to **steel** to make parts of an **aircraft** that become very hot.
Many of the jet engine's parts were made of titanium steel.

toaster *noun*
A toaster is an **appliance** for toasting bread. It contains wires that are heated by an **electric current**. The bread is placed close to the wires. When the toast is ready, a **spring** makes it pop up and switches off the current.
He made them each a slice of toast in the toaster.

toboggan *noun*
A toboggan is a long, narrow **sled** usually made from wood or a hard **plastic**. It is used to travel downhill on a snow-covered slope. The base of the toboggan is flat and smooth, and the front curves upward. Unlike a sled, it has no runners. A toboggan often has side rails.
Native American peoples have used toboggans for thousands of years.

tool *noun*
A tool is a **device** for carrying out a particular task. **Hammers, planes, wrenches,** and **screwdrivers** are tools. Tools powered by **motors** are called **power** tools. **Electric drills** and **circular saws** are power tools.
The mechanic kept all his tools in a toolbox so that he could carry them around when he was working.

torpedo *noun*
A torpedo is a weapon fired at sea by a **warship**. It has its own **motor**. A torpedo is fired underwater toward the hull of an enemy **ship**. When it reaches its target, a warhead in the nose of the torpedo explodes.
Many enemy ships were sunk by torpedoes fired by submarines.

torque *noun*
Torque is the **force** an **engine** uses to turn a **shaft**. A large torque is needed to start an engine moving. Once it is moving, less torque is needed to keep it going. A **vehicle** uses torque from its engine to turn the **wheels**.
The heavy truck needed a large torque to pull away from the curb.

tower crane *noun*
A tower crane is a kind of **crane** used on building sites. It is a tall, metal tower with a crossbar, or jib, at the top. The crane driver can swing the jib in any direction. **Cables** hang from one end of the jib and there is a **counterweight** at the other end.
The tower crane lifted slabs of concrete and put them in place.

track *noun*
1. A track is a collection of rails and switches on a railway line.
The train came quickly down the track.
2. A track is a place where events such as car and motorcycle races are held.
The racing car skidded and came off the track.

traction engine *noun*
A traction engine is a kind of tractor or locomotive that is driven by a steam engine. Traction engines can be used to pull wagons, plows or other machines along roads or over fields.
Traction engines can also operate other machines if the drive of the engine is connected by an endless belt to the machine.

tractor ► page 144

traffic lights *plural noun*
Traffic lights are **signals**. They tell road users when it is safe to move on. They show a red light for danger, green for safety, and an amber light which means caution. Traffic lights are usually found on busy roads and in towns and cities.
The traffic lights were red, so the bus stopped.

train *noun*
A train is a **vehicle** that runs along a **track**. It is usually made up of several cars. Trains are pulled or pushed by locomotives **powered** by **steam engines**, **diesel engines**, or **electric motors**. They are often used for carrying passengers and moving freight. Trains may also be used beneath the streets for underground roads called subways.
We went to the railroad station to catch the early train.

transceiver *noun*
A transceiver is a **device** with an **aerial**, which can both **transmit** and receive messages by **radio**. It is small enough to fit into a pocket. Police and other emergency services often use transceivers to relay and receive important messages.
At the scene of the accident, the policeman took his transceiver out of his pocket and spoke to headquarters.

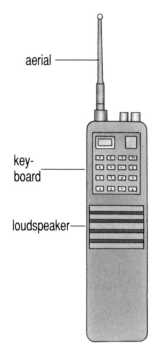

aerial

keyboard

loudspeaker

transducer *noun*
A transducer is a **device** that changes energy from one form to another. A **microphone** is a transducer because it changes sound energy into electrical energy. **Phototransistors**, **light bulbs**, **loudspeakers**, and **solenoids** are some other kinds of transducers.
All forms of telecommunications rely on transducers to make them work.

transformer *noun*
A transformer is a **device** that makes an **electric current** stronger or weaker. It is made of two separate **coils** of wire that are wound onto an **iron** core.
The transformer decreased the current from the power station from 15,000 volts to 220 volts.

transistor *noun*
A transistor is an **electronic device** made from a material called silicon. Transistors have three wires attached to them, which allows the strength or direction of **electric signals** to be changed.
Radios, television sets, and record players all contain transistors.

tractor *noun*

A tractor is a **vehicle** that is used mainly on farms. It can do many different jobs. Tractors can pull wagons and farm **machines**, such as **plows**. With **power takeoff** they can also provide energy for other machines.
The farmer connected his tractor to a plow and set off to plow his land.

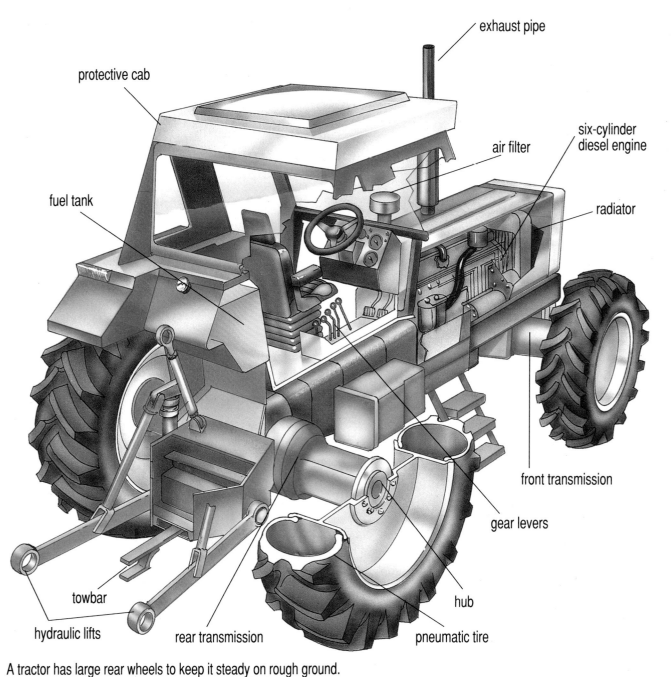

exhaust pipe

protective cab

six-cylinder diesel engine

air filter

fuel tank

radiator

front transmission

gear levers

towbar

hub

hydraulic lifts

rear transmission

pneumatic tire

A tractor has large rear wheels to keep it steady on rough ground. Its tires have deep treads to grip well in muddy fields.

transmission   *noun*
A transmission is part of a **vehicle** driven by an **engine**. It is made up of **gears**. The transmission sends, or **transmits**, energy from the engine's **drive shaft** to the **wheels**.
The car's transmission was faulty and it broke down.

transmit   *verb*
Transmit means to carry or send something from one place to another. In a car, energy is transmitted from the **engine** to the driving **wheels**. A **radio transmitter** transmits **electric signals** to **radio receivers**.
A telephone transmits and receives voice messages.

transmitter   *noun*
A transmitter is a **device** that sends out **electric signals** by means of **radio waves**. **Radio** and **television** signals come from transmitters. A television **antenna receives** and turns them into electric signals. A **tuner** picks a signal, which is then **amplified** and split into picture and sound signals.
The radio signals that we picked up were very faint because we were a long way from the transmitter.

transport   *verb*
To transport is to move people or things from one place to another. Early people transported things on foot. When the wheel was invented people could transport themselves and goods by wheeled vehicles such as wagons. Boats allow transportation across water, and today planes allow transportation by air.
You can transport mail quickly by air.

treadle   *noun*
A treadle is a part of a **machine** that uses **power** from a human foot to turn a **wheel**. A person presses the treadle up and down, which causes the machine to operate. Some **sewing machines** and small **lathes** are operated by a treadle.
She worked the treadle and began to sew.

tumble dryer   *noun*
A tumble dryer is an **appliance** for drying wet laundry. It contains a **heater** and an **electric motor**. The clothes are placed in a drum, which is turned, or **rotated**, by the motor. As it rotates, warm air flows through the contents of the drum and dries them.
Our clothes were soaked by the rain, so we put them in the tumble dryer.

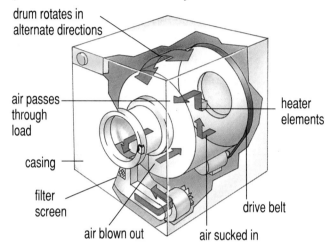

drum rotates in alternate directions

air passes through load

casing

filter screen

air blown out

heater elements

drive belt

air sucked in

tuner   *noun*
A tuner is part of a **hi-fi** system. It selects the **radio** frequency that has the program you want to hear. It has an **aerial**, an **amplifier**, and **loudspeakers**.
A tuner may be adjusted by turning a knob.

turbine   *noun*
A turbine is a **machine**. Its **shaft** is connected to a set of curved blades separated by slits. A **gas** or liquid flows against the blades and through the slits, which causes the blades to turn, or **rotate**. This in turn spins the shaft of the turbine. Some ships are powered by turbines.
Turbines are used in power stations.

turbocharger   *noun*
A turbocharger is a part of some **internal combustion engines**. It uses **exhaust gases** from the engine to drive a **turbine**. This runs another turbine, which forces more air into the engine.
A turbocharger makes a car's engine very powerful.

145

turbofan *noun*
A turbofan is a kind of **jet engine**. It contains a **turbine**, which is called a **fan**. This allows a blanket of air around the inside of the engine to be forced out through special jets. Turbofan engines are more efficient and quieter than other jet engines. They are sometimes called fanjets.
The airliner had turbofan engines and so it took off quietly.

turbojet *noun*
A turbojet is a kind of **jet engine**. It has a **compressor** that compresses the air entering the intake. This **compressed air** is mixed with **fuel** and set alight, or ignited. The **force** of hot **gases** being pushed out of the **exhaust** drives the engine forward.
The airliner was powered by four turbojets.

turnstile *noun*
A turnstile is a **device** that counts the number of people passing through a gate. Each person passing through moves a **lever**, which operates a counter. Turnstiles are used at stadiums and in some supermarkets.
There was a crowd waiting to go through the turnstiles at the football game.

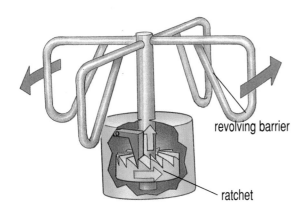
revolving barrier
ratchet

turntable *noun*
A turntable is a circular platform that **rotates**. Railroad locomotives are sometimes turned around on turntables. The turntable of a **record player** makes the record rotate.
Railroad turntables are built very solidly.

turning tool *noun*
A turning tool is a **tool** that is used to shape objects on a **lathe**. Turning tools include cutters, scrapers, and polishers. They are made of hardened **steel**.
He used turning tools to shape the leg of the chair with his lathe.

tweezers *plural noun*
Tweezers are small **tools** that are used for very accurate work with small objects. They have two jaws that are squeezed together to pick up objects.
Watchmakers use tweezers when they make or repair watches.

twin-rotor helicopter *noun*
A twin-rotor helicopter is a large **helicopter** with two sets of **rotor blades** mounted above the **fuselage**. Twin-rotor helicopters used by soldiers are sometimes called helicopter gunships.
There were many passengers on board the twin-rotor helicopter.

two-stroke engine *noun*
A two-stroke engine is an **internal combustion engine**. Each stroke moves a **piston** up or down inside a **cylinder** to create **power**. The **fuel** and air enter the cylinder through a slot in the cylinder wall. The **exhaust gas** leaves through another slot. There are only two moving parts in a two-stroke engine, the piston and the **crank**.
Small motorcycles often have two-stroke engines.

typesetting machines *noun*
Typesetting machines are **machines** that lay out type for printing. Some typesetting machines use molten metal that is poured into molds. Modern typesetting machines are similar to **word processors**. They produce printed sheets called camera-ready copy. This is **photographed** and made into a printing plate.
At the newspaper office, the news was being set into type by typesetting machines.

typewriter *noun*
A typewriter is a **machine** that produces
printed letters and numbers. It is operated
by pressing **keys** on a **keyboard**. The type
is on separate metal bars, on a daisy-wheel,
or on a round, metal ball that is called a
"golfball." A typewriter can be operated by
hand or **powered** by an **electric motor**.
He typed the letter on his typewriter.

ultrasound scanner *noun*
An ultrasound scanner is a **device** used in
hospitals to examine inside the body. An
ultrasound scanner sends **very-high-
frequency** sound waves into the body and
records the echoes. It works in a way similar
to **sonar**. The results can be viewed on a
television screen or a printout.
*The doctor used an ultrasound scanner to
study her patient's heart.*

undercarriage ► landing gear

uranium *noun*
Uranium is a very heavy metal that is used
in **nuclear reactors**. It makes the energy on
which **nuclear power stations** run. Uranium
also gives off dangerous radiation.
*Uranium must be handled with great care
because it can damage living tissues.*

147

vacuum *noun*

A vacuum is a space that contains no material of any kind. Liquids and **gases** try to fill a vacuum if they can. Vacuums are used in some **pumps**. A complete vacuum can be found only in outer space.
A vacuum flask or jug is a glass container surrounded by a vacuum, to keep liquid hot or cold.

vacuum cleaner *noun*

A vacuum cleaner is an **appliance** that is used in the home. It contains a **fan** that makes a partial **vacuum** inside the body of the cleaner. Air from outside rushes in to fill the vacuum, and dust and dirt are sucked in with it.
He used a vacuum cleaner to clean up.

valve *noun*

A valve is a **device** that controls the flow of a liquid or **gas** through an opening. It can be opened or shut. Some valves allow a liquid or gas to flow in only one direction. A water **tap** is a kind of valve.
The plumber turned a valve in the basement to stop the flow of water which could have flooded the kitchen.

VCR ► video cassette recorder

VDU ► visual display unit

vehicle *noun*

A vehicle is a **machine** for traveling over land. Cars, trucks, **tractors**, and vans are all kinds of vehicles. They are **powered** by **internal combustion engines** that use either **gasoline** or **diesel fuel**. Some vehicles have **electric motors**.
The vehicle sped by us.

vending machine *noun*

A vending machine is a **machine** that automatically supplies goods when money is put into a slot.
Vending machines can stock candy, hot or cold drinks, sandwiches, and other goods.

vertical-takeoff-and-landing aircraft
noun

A vertical-takeoff-and-landing aircraft, or VTOL, is an **airplane** that can take off and land without a runway, or with only a very short runway. VTOLs have **engines** with **jets** that can be turned sideways or downward to provide **power** for turning or rising. Vertical-takeoff-and-landing aircraft are sometimes used on a type of **warship** called an **aircraft** carrier.
A jump jet is a vertical-takeoff-and-landing aircraft.

very-high-frequency   *adjective*
Very-high-frequency describes some radio
or sound waves. Very-high-frequency **radio
waves** carry **radio** and **television** signals.
Very high frequency sound waves are used
in **sonar** and **ultrasound scanners**. The
abbreviation for very high frequency is VHF.
*The policemen talked to each other on their
very-high-frequency radios.*

video camera ► **television camera**

video cassette recorder   *noun*
A video cassette recorder is a **machine**
which records and plays back moving
pictures and sound.
*A video cassette recorder is useful for
recording television programs to watch later.*

videotape   *noun*
Videotape is special tape with tracks that
have been magnetized so that they react to
electrical impulses. These record both
sounds and pictures on the tape.
Play the videotape of the Beatles' concert.

vise   *noun*
A vise is a **tool** that grips objects on which
work is being done. Its grip is made tighter
or looser by turning a **lever**. The lever is
attached to a **shaft** that has a thread like a
bolt.
*The carpenter put the piece of wood in a
vise so that it would not move around while
he was planing it.*

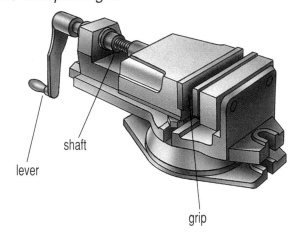

shaft

lever

grip

visual display unit   *noun*
A visual display unit, or VDU for short, is a
part of a **computer**. It has a **screen** similar
to the screen of a **television set**. The
screen shows **data** that are typed on a
keyboard, as well as the work that the
computer has done.
*He pressed a key and new data appeared
on the visual display unit.*

VTOL ► **vertical-takeoff-and-landing
aircraft**

warhead *noun*

A warhead is a part of a **bomb**, **torpedo**, or **missile**. It contains an explosive that is set on fire, or detonated, when the warhead reaches the target. Modern explosives are harmless until a detonator is attached.
Some submarines can fire missiles with nuclear warheads.

warship ► page 152

washer *noun*

1. A washer is a small, flat **disk** of metal or fiber with a hole in the center. A **bolt** passes through the hole and a **nut** is threaded onto the bolt. The washer holds the nut and bolt tightly together.
The nut worked loose because he had forgotten to put a washer on the bolt.
2. A washer is a part of a **tap** or **valve**. It is made of a soft material such as rubber that can be squeezed. A washer stops a liquid or **gas** from leaking through a closed tap or valve.
The plumber came to put in a new washer because the bathroom sink was leaking.

washing machine *noun*

A washing machine is an **appliance** that washes the laundry automatically. The laundry is placed in a drum with detergent. The drum fills with water and turns back and forth. When the laundry is clean, it is rinsed and the water is **pumped** out. Some washing machines contain a **spin dryer** or a **tumble dryer**.
They collected the family's dirty clothes and put them in the washing machine.

watch   *noun*

A watch is a **device** for telling the time. Most watches are worn on the wrist. Some have a **clockwork motor** and others are driven by **electricity** from a tiny button **battery**.
He looked at his watch and saw that he was going to be late.

water-cooled   *adjective*

Water-cooled describes a **machine** that has cool water flowing round it to prevent it from becoming too hot. A series of pipes carry the water around a water-cooled machine. A **fan** is often used to keep the water cool. Most **internal combustion engines** are water-cooled.
He filled the car's radiator to stop the water-cooled engine from overheating.

water gauge   *noun*

A water gauge is a **device** for measuring the depth of water in a **vessel**, such as a tank.
He checked the level in the kettle by looking at the water guage.

water turbine   *noun*

A water turbine is a **machine**. It has a **shaft** that is driven by water flowing through the slits between the turbine blades. Most water turbines are driven by water that is stored behind dams, or from waterfalls. Water turbines are found in **hydroelectric power** stations. They are also known as hydraulic turbines.
Water from the fast-flowing river provided energy to turn the water turbine.

waterwheel   *noun*

A waterwheel is a **wheel** that is made to turn by flowing water. Blades stand out from the **hub** of the waterwheel so that the water falls onto them.
Waterwheels can be used to drive pumps and other machines.

wave power ► **tidal power**

weaving machine ► **loom**

web offset printing press   *noun*

A web offset printing press is a **machine** that prints by **offset lithography**. It prints onto a reel of paper called a web. The printed web is then passed through a dryer and into a folder, which cuts and folds the paper. This produces folded sections that are bound together.
Most newspapers are printed on web offset printing presses.

weighing machine ► page 154

weigh station   *noun*

A weigh station is a place where **vehicles** and their **loads** are weighed. The vehicle is driven onto a platform. The platform sinks with the vehicle and the amount it sinks is shown on a **dial** giving the weight of the vehicle.
The driver drove his truck onto the scale at the weigh station.

warship *noun*

A warship is a **ship** designed to take part in war. **Frigates**, destroyers, **aircraft** carriers, and most **submarines** are kinds of warships.

There were several naval warships docked at the port.

An aircraft carrier is the largest and most powerful warship. It has a flight deck with special equipment that allows aircraft, such as fighter and bomber planes, to take off and land without a runway. Aircraft carriers also carry helicopters and other kinds of small planes.

A frigate is used mainly to defend other ships against enemy submarines. They carry anti-submarine weapons, such as torpedoes and nuclear depth charges.

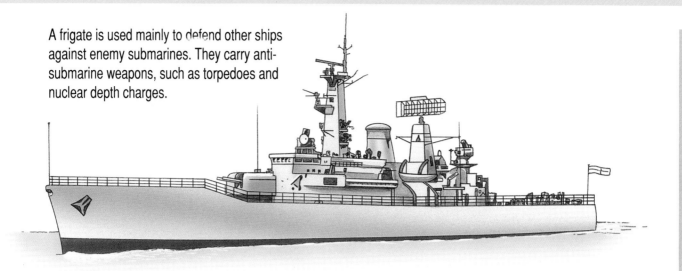

A patrol boat is a small warship. It is used to guard rivers and coastal waters.

A destroyer carries guns, missiles and anti-submarine weapons. It defends other ships and also carries out search and rescue missions at sea.

weighing machine   *noun*

A weighing machine is a **machine** that measures the weight of objects.
Kitchen scales, and spring balances are kinds of weighing machines.

A French mathematician named Roberval designed this weighing machine in 1669. It weighs objects accurately by means of two pans. The object to be weighed is placed in one pan and weights are placed in the other to balance the object. Simple kitchen scales are based on this design.

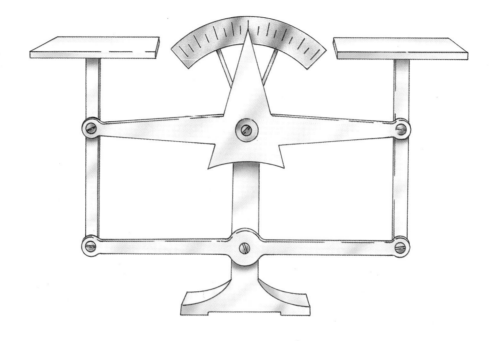

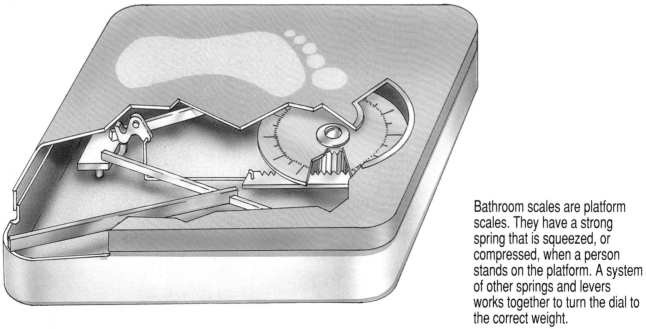

Bathroom scales are platform scales. They have a strong spring that is squeezed, or compressed, when a person stands on the platform. A system of other springs and levers works together to turn the dial to the correct weight.

These scales have a spring mechanism inside, which moves the hand on the dial when a weight is placed in the pan.

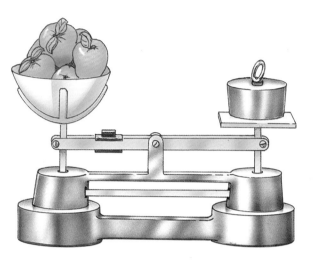

This simple design using two pans and weights was based on Roberval's weighing machine.

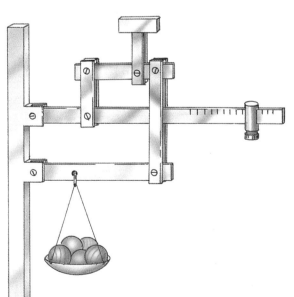

These platform scales use a system of levers connected together by vertical bars. The main lever has a scale marked on it and a sliding weight. An object is placed on the platform. The main lever moves up and the weight is slid along the scale until all the levers balance.

This spring balance is useful for weighing awkward objects, such as heavy suitcases. An object is hung on the hook, which pulls down a very strong spring. This moves the marker on the scale to show the object's weight.

wheel *noun*

A wheel is a **disk** that turns, or rotates, around a **shaft** or **axle**. **Bicycles**, cars, and trucks travel on wheels that are fitted with rubber **tires**. **Gears** are wheels with **cogs**. *Most cars have four wheels, and most motorcycles have two.*

The first wheels known to have been used on vehicles were made with three planks of wood joined by wooden struts. The Sumerians used such wheels about 5,000 years ago on their chariots.

Wheels were probably first used thousands of years ago for making pottery. Today, potters' wheels are sometimes turned by electric motors.

A modern bicycle wheel is made of aluminum, which is strong but very lightweight. Thin metal spokes support the outer rim.

Waterwheels are still used in some countries to drive simple machines.

Some road vehicles have huge wheels to carry them over rough ground.

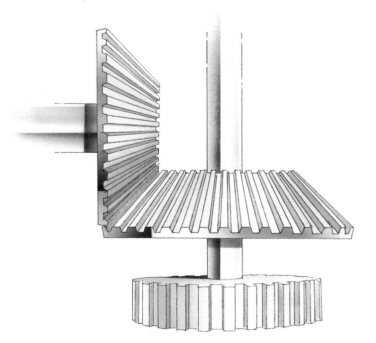

Gearwheels, such as this bevel gear, are used in many machines to pass, or transmit, energy from one part to another.

welding *noun*
Welding is a method of joining pieces of metal. The usual method of welding is to melt the edges of the metal so that they join together, or fuse, without a break.
The parts of a car body are joined by welding.
weld *verb*

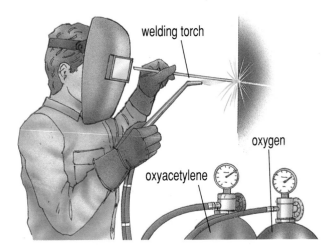

welding torch

oxygen

oxyacetylene

welding torch *noun*
A welding torch is a **tool** that produces a very hot flame used to **weld** pieces of metal together. The flame comes from burning gases, usually oxygen and acetylene.
The mechanic used a welding torch to repair the broken metal part.

wheel ► page 156

wheel and axle *noun*
A wheel and axle is a simple machine that uses a cylindrical axle onto which a rope is fastened. The axle is turned by a handle to shorten or lengthen the rope. Any weight fastened to the rope is easily raised or lowered using this device.
An old-fashioned well used a wheel and axle to raise the bucket of water.

wheelbarrow *noun*
A wheelbarrow is a **simple machine** used by builders and gardeners. It is a kind of **lever**.
A wheelbarrow allows a person to do more work than could be done by lifting and carrying.

wheelchair *noun*
A chair mounted on wheels is known as a wheelchair. It is used especially by disabled people and can be moved and turned using special controls that are attached to one of the arms.
She lowered herself down the ramp from the ambulance in her wheelchair.

whisk *noun*
A whisk is a **device** used in cooking. It is used to mix the whites and yolks of eggs and for many other purposes. A whisk can either be operated by hand or by an **electric motor**.
He used a whisk to beat the eggs to make an omelet.

winch *noun*
A winch is a **simple machine** for lifting objects. It is operated by turning a **wheel** with a handle. A rope is wound around the wheel and hooked onto the object being lifted. Winches are used mostly for lifting heavy objects.
They hauled the boat up the ramp with a winch.

windmill *noun*
A windmill is a **machine** that makes use of **wind power**. It has blades or sails, which are driven around by the wind. Many years ago, windmills were used to grind wheat into flour.
The sails of the windmill drove a shaft, which turned and made the grindstone move.

wind power *noun*
Wind power is the use of wind to **generate electricity** or operate **machines**. The wind can spin a **turbine** or a **propeller**. In this way, wind energy is changed to electrical or **mechanical energy**. Wind power, together with solar power and water power, are forms of alternative energy.
Scientists hope that one day more electricity will be generated by wind power, because it does not harm the environment.

windshield wiper *noun*
A windshield wiper is a **device** that clears rain and dirt from the windshield of a **vehicle**. It has one or more blades driven by an **electric motor**.
It was raining hard, so the driver switched on the windshield wipers.

wind turbine *noun*
A wind turbine is a **machine** that **generates electricity** by using **wind power**. The wind blows through the blades of a small **turbine**, which is connected to a **generator**. Electricity is produced when the turbine blades **rotate**. Most wind turbines are mounted on a swivel on top of a tower. This means that they can be turned to face the wind when it changes direction.
Wind turbines work well if they are built in places where there are strong winds.

worm gear *noun*
A worm gear is a part of some **machines**. Unlike other **gears**, a worm gear has a continuous thread, like a **screw**. A **gearwheel** turns a second gearwheel called a worm, set at right angles to the first.
Worm gears change the direction of a drive by 90 degrees.

wrench *noun*
A wrench is a **tool** that is used to turn a **nut** or **bolt**. It has a notch cut in the end that is the same size as the nut or the head of the bolt. Wrenches are made of **steel**.
He used a wrench to tighten the nut on his bicycle.

X-ray *noun*
An X-ray is a **very-high-frequency electromagnetic** wave. X-ray **machines** can show the insides of bodies. Doctors use X-rays to inspect patients' lungs and to check for broken bones.
After his fall, he went to the hospital for an X-ray to check that no bones were broken.

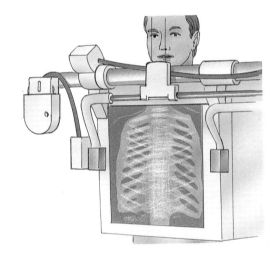

zoom lens   *noun*

A zoom lens is a **camera lens** that can be adjusted for close-up or distant **photographs** while keeping the object in focus all the time. It is made up of a number of lenses.

Zoom lenses are used with still, television, and movie cameras.

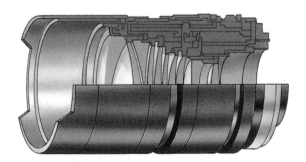